# DAVID BAKER'S

# JAZZ IMPROVISATION

## A Comprehensive Method for All Musicians

## REVISED EDITION

Alfred
ap

# Table of Contents

# FOREWORD

It was inevitable that, with the inroads made by jazz into academia in recent years, numerous methods and analytic studies of one kind or another would appear to aid the student and the teacher. In this growing body of jazz literature, the present volume stands out as one of the most useful and most sorely needed.

Mr. Baker's experience, both as a player and a teacher, and his long list of creative and educational accomplishments on behalf of jazz, make him an ideal "interpreter" of the musical, technical problems the young jazz improvisor faces and how most effectively to solve them. Perhaps the outstanding quality of the book is its comprehensiveness. Many aspects of jazz are dealt with at both the fundamental and most sophisticated levels. It is a particular pleasure to see — for once — the dramatic and psychological aspects of jazz improvisation treated in a methodical, practical, no-nonsense manner.

Inevitably, a method can only suggest and prod, and provide some tools; it can never substitute for the real playing experience in an ensemble or performance context. But the lessons with respect to communicating with an audience, the structuring of the "dramatic" content of a solo — above and beyond technique and merely "running the changes" — lessons young musicians used to learn on the road in the bands or at jam sessions — are dealt with, perhaps for the first time, by an experienced musician who **values** these aspects of jazz improvisation and moreover is able to analyze and "teach" them.

The design and format of the book is simple and practical, combining verbal explication with musical exercise material. In its range, covering everything from the most elementary problems of nomenclature through fundamental exercises in improvisation techniques all the way to advanced concepts of jazz playing, Mr. Baker's book should prove to be a most useful addition to the literature.

*Gunther Schuller*
Tanglewood

# PREFACE

This book addresses itself to the needs of the teacher, student, amateur and professional musician alike. I know of few jazz musicians who could not profit from disciplined studies in some of the areas covered in this book. Teachers and students are in dire need of some guidelines for studying the disciplines of jazz improvisation.

By and large, college and high school teachers involved in jazz studies have hopelessly inadequate backgrounds in jazz. Many times the teacher's only qualification will be a love for jazz. While this love may constitute a sufficient background upon which to learn, it is not, however, a sufficient one from which to teach.

Some would argue against teaching improvisation since most players will probably be section players in a band if they pursue jazz at all. Knowledge of improvisation is an absolute necessity if one is to do a first class job anywhere in a jazz band. Knowing something of improvisation is bound to provide insights that will improve the quality of the student's playing.

If we accept the assumption that the essence of jazz is improvisation, then steps must be taken to assure this as the end result. A step toward such an end would be to establish the importance of, and need for, courses in the art of improvising. The fact that this need has grown during the last twenty years can be attributed to a number of things.

First, the increasing harmonic, rhythmic, and structural complexities of contemporary jazz make it virtually impossible for the novice, who would play well, to find his way around without some professional help.

Some twenty years ago, when blues, tunes with "I Got Rhythm" changes, and standards comprised the greater portion of the jazz repertoire, it was conceivable that a player might achieve competency without requiring help in a formal sense, such as schools, etc. Now, however, with increasing technical and musical demands born of advanced and rapidly growing compositional skills, courses in improvisation assume a position of utmost importance. There probably are few novices who don't approach, without some trepidation, vertical structures such as John Coltrane's "Giant Steps" or Benny Golson's "Stablemates", or compositionally difficult structures such as George Russell's "The Outer View" or "D.C. Divertimento".

Another reason these improvising courses are so important is the ever decreasing number of jam sessions. In past years, jam sessions served as a kind of practical school for budding musicians. Here they could learn tunes, experiment, exchange ideas, and, in general, grow musically. However, this institution is fast approaching extinction, at least in its old-fashioned and most rewarding form.

The diversification of jazz today is another reason for the increasing importance of improvisation courses. Never before have there been so many divergent schools of jazz thought coexisting and enjoying concurrent popularity — blues, swing, traditional, avant-garde, third stream, eclectics, and myriad offshoots of those — that a student must be made aware of if he is to find his niche.

Last, a new-found awareness of the vast resources and materials available to the jazz musician have made improvisation courses indispensable to the conscientious student who would derive maximum benefit from these resources.

Some suggestions for using this book.

1. Whether used by a beginner or an advanced player, all chapters should be covered. The material in every chapter is designed to suit the needs of all players and differs for the individual player only in degree of difficulty.

2. Much of the material can be studied as necessity demands and need not occur in the order suggested in the book. It is, however, my recommendation that everyone be completely comfortable with the materials in chapters one and two before going further.

3. The player should make extended use of the list of recorded materials at the end of each chapter.

4. The player should read as many of the books suggested as possible. Many of them are probably available in the local library, others can be purchased inexpensively in paperback editions.

5. The player should make use of the written examples. He should play them on his instrument. He should try to recognize them when other players use them.

6. The player should try to use the materials in every chapter in a musical manner. He should strive to use the material in a manner consistent with his personal convictions. However, he should not let his imagination and ingenuity be stifled by fear of the unfamiliar.

7. **The player must always try to bring something of his personality to every musical situation!!!**

*David Baker*
Bloomington, Indiana

# PREFACE TO THE REVISED EDITION

This long overdue revision of *Jazz Improvisation* is the result of a number of factors, among them the following:

(1) Fifteen years of constant contact with thousands of students from all over the world — students ranging from absolute beginners to top professionals, from the marginally talented to the supertalented; students from seven years of age to seventy years of age; performers on virtually every instrument; those who wanted to play solely for their enjoyment to those who would ultimately become top professionals; students from every background, from college and conservatory-trained youngsters to thoroughly sophisticated studio professionals and intuitive street players

(2) Continued growth through years of teaching shoulder to shoulder with many of the finest teachers in the world today

(3) Performing with many of jazz's greatest practitioners on a regular basis

(4) Composing for and working with the world's top musicians

(5) A relentless and tireless re-examination of both the content and the methodology of jazz teaching

(6) Continued access to a seemingly endless stream of both new recordings and reissues

(7) Access to new information and new perspectives and insights about extant information

(8) Enlightened and more imaginative ways of communicating said information

(9) A generally more sophisticated and receptive environment with regard to jazz scholarship

This revision includes a number of completely new chapters (though often under their original titles), new and updated bibliographic and discographic information (purging of out-of-print materials and replacing of much material with better, more relevant, and more accessible material), and the reordering of much of the information to make the book easier to use (for example, placing all of the musical examples directly after the material being exemplified). In terms of material it is one fourth larger, but because of more efficient use of space and a more compact format, it is smaller and more easily used.

*David N. Baker*
Bloomington, Indiana

# Chapter I

# NOMENCLATURE

One of the first things that an aspiring jazz musician must do is learn to read and interpret chord symbols. The six chord types are major, minor, dominant, diminished, augmented, and half diminished.

An alphabetical letter indicates the root on which a chord is built. The tertian system is usually employed, that is, chords are built in consecutive thirds (i.e., C-E-G-B-D-F-A). For the uninitiated two short cuts to aid in chord construction follow: (1) build the chord using alternating letters of the musical alphabet (i.e., F-A-C-E-G-B-D-etc.) and (2) build the chord using either the lines E-G-B-D-F or the spaces F-A-C-E.

In the major chord types all notes are indigenous to the major scale of the root tone, i.e. C major is spelled C-E-G-B-D-etc., Eb major is spelled Eb-G-Bb-D-F-etc., and so forth. Numerically this can be expressed 1-3-5-7-9-11-etc. A letter standing alone usually indicates a major triad, which is a chord consisting of the root, the major third, and the perfect fifth, i.e., C-E-G, F-A-C, Gb-Bb-Db, etc.

All major type chords have the word "major" or one of the symbols of abbreviation in the title with the exception of the triad (i.e., C-E-G) and the chord of the added sixth (i.e., $C_6$=C-E-G-A). The term extension refers to the notes higher than the seventh in a tertian structure, i.e., the ninth, eleventh, thirteenth, etc. We may extend the major chord by using the letter names of the major scale built on the root of the chord (i.e., Ab major 13, which is spelled Ab-C-Eb-G-Bb-Db-F) or by using the unaltered odd numbers (1-3-5-7-9-11-13). The most commonly used symbols and abbreviations for major are Maj, Ma, M, $\triangle$ , a letter by itself, and a letter plus the number six, i.e., the following: C Maj, C Ma, C M, C $\triangle$ , C, and $C_6$. In abbreviations for major use a capital letter M for the first letter of the abbreviation.

All minor type chords have the word minor (use small letter m) or one of the symbols or abbreviations for minor in the title with the exception of the half diminished chord. For our purposes the half diminished chord is better called a minor seventh with a flat five ($mi_7^{(b5)}$). The most commonly used symbols and abbreviations for minor are min, mi, m, and–, i.e., the following: C min, C mi, C m, and C–. To this we may add the numbers which indicate the members of the scale to be added, i.e., C mi 11, which is spelled C-Eb-G-Bb-D-F.

In constructing a minor chord we again think of the root of the chord as being the tonic note of a major scale. We then lower the third of the chord one half step. The resultant triad is indicated by a letter plus the word minor or one of its abbreviations. To this triad we may add the lowered or minor seventh. The spelling is then 1-b3-5-b7; if we use the note C as the root of the chord, C $mi_7$ is spelled C-Eb-G-Bb. Any extensions added to the minor chord are indigenous to the major scale of the root tone; C mi 11 is spelled, for example, C-Eb-G-Bb-D-F or 1-b3-5-b7-9-11.

An altered chord tone or extension is indicated by a plus (+) or sharp (#) for raised and by a minus (–) or flat (b) for lowered. Altered and added notes are best parenthesized to avoid confusion, i.e., $C_7^{(b9)}$, $C_7^{(add\ 4)}$, and $Cmi_7^{(b9)}$

The dominant seventh chord is constructed as follows: 1-3-5-b7, or, in other words, lower the seventh of the major scale of the root one half step (using C as the root, the chord is spelled C-E-G-Bb). The number seven, unless accompanied by the word major or minor, means to add the minor seventh to the triad. Any letter plus a number other than six signifies a dominant seventh chord, i.e. the following: $C_9$ is spelled C-E-G-Bb-D; $C_{13}$ is spelled C-E-G-Bb-D-F-A. All extensions are indigenous to the major key of the root tone, i.e. the following: $C_{13}$ is spelled C-E-G-Bb-D-F-A.

The diminished chord is constructed 1-b3-b5-6; using C as the root the chord is spelled C-Eb-Gb-A. In jazz all references to a diminished chord mean diminished seventh. In this chord all adjacent members are a minor third apart. The symbol for diminished is a circle; its abbreviation is dim. (small letter d).

The augmented chord is constructed 1-3-#5; using C as the root the chord is spelled C-E-G#. In this chord all adjacent members are a major third apart. The symbol for augmented is a plus sign (+); its abbreviation is aug.

The half diminished chord is also known as a minor seventh with a flat five ($mi_7^{(b5)}$) and is constructed 1-b3-b5-b7; using C as the root the chord is spelled C-Eb-Gb-Bb. The half diminished chord is symbolized ø and abbreviated $mi_7^{(b5)}$.

All chords that are neither major nor minor function as dominant seventh chords, i.e., C+, $C_{13}$, $Co_7$, $C_{11}$, etc. The augmented chord usually functions as the dominant seventh chord with the same root name, i.e., C+=$C_7$(+5). Diminished chords are usually derived dominant seventh chords. The root tone is found a major third below the bottom tone of the diminished chord, i.e., $Co_7$=$Ab_7$.

1

One of the most perplexing problems for beginning jazz players is reconciling the key signature of a composition to the seeming inconsistencies in the realizations of the chord symbols, i.e., the following examples:

Why is there no Eb in this chord?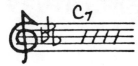

Why is there no F# in this chord?

In answering these questions observe the following rule: the key signature of a composition has no direct bearing on the spelling of individual chords. The symbols dictate the realization of the chord.

Properly interpreting the chord of the added sixth poses another problem for many people because this chord is often an inverted form of a minor seventh chord. This problem should be handled as follows: if the chord of the added sixth resolves to a dominant seventh chord a major second above or a dominant seventh chord a major third below its root, it should be treated as a minor seventh chord. To locate its root, invert the chord until it is arranged in thirds, i.e., the following: $C_6$ (C-E-G-A) = $Ami_7$ and $Ebmi_6$ (Eb-Gb-Bb-C) = $C\emptyset_7$.

SUMMARY: Information for determining chord categories

## CHORD TYPES

Major: 1-3-5-7-9-etc.

Minor: 1-b3-5-b7-9-etc.

Dominant: 1-3-5-b7-9-etc.

Diminished: 1-b3-b5-6

Half diminished: 1-b3-b5-b7

Augmented: 1-3-#5

## ABBREVIATIONS (using C as root)

C, C △ , C Major, C $Maj_7$, C Ma, C $Ma_7$, $C_7$, C $Maj_7$, C M, C $M_7$

C-, $C-_7$, C min, C $min_7$, Cmi, $Cmi_7$, Cm, $Cm_7$

$C_7$, $C_9$, $C_{11}$, $C_{13}$

Co, $Co_7$, C dim, C $dim_7$

$C\emptyset$, $Cmi_7^{(b5)}$, $C-^{(b5)}$

C+, $C_7+$, $C_7^{\#5}$, $C_7$ aug, $C_7^{+5}$

Alterations and additions are made according to the key of the bottom tone.

## CHORD CATEGORIES

I:   All major type chords (i.e., C, $C_6$, all chords with major in the title)
II:  All minor type chords (minor in the title) including the $\emptyset_7$
V:   Any dominant seventh chord (letter plus a number other than 6); anything other than a major or minor type
Special V chord types: (1) Augmented (Aug=dominant 7th of the same name, i.e., $C+=C_7$)
(2) Diminished. Diminished chords are usually derived from the dominant 7th a major third below the root of the diminished chord, i.e., $Co_7=Ab_7$.

## SOME SUGGESTED EXERCISES

1.   Name the six chord types and give examples of each.
2.   Give an example of an extension to an $Ab_7$ chord.
3.   Build the following chords:

   a.   Ab 13

   b.   $G_7^{(+11)}$

   c.   $Dmi_9$

   d.   E

   e.   $A\emptyset_7$

   f.   $D_9^{(b11)}$

   g.   $Fo_7$

   h.   $Bbmi_7^{(b5)}$

   i.   $C_7 \left( {}^{\#9}_{\#5} \right)$

   j.   F#

2

4. Classify the chords in exercise #3 as to major, minor, or dominant function.
5. Give the dominant 7th to which the following diminished chords belong:
    a. $Ao_7$
    b. $Do_7$
    c. $F\#o_7$
    d. $Bo_7$
    e. $Co_7$
6. Find the roots of the following chords:
    a. C-E-G-A
    b. B-E-G-A-C
    c. Db-Ab-Bb-F-Gb-Eb
    d. $F\#$-C-Eb-A
    e. E-B-D-G

# Chapter II

# FOUNDATION EXERCISES FOR THE JAZZ PLAYER

The playing of jazz presupposes a certain skill with scales and chords. This chapter will contain some suggestions for exercises designed to develop this basic skill. Each person should use the scales and chord patterns in a manner consistent with his ability and state of development.

In practicing scales and chords observe the following general rule. **All scales should be practiced starting on the lowest note on the instrument contained in that scale.** For instance, if the lowest note on the instrument is an F# and the A Major scale is being played, start on the note F#; if playing a C scale, start on the note G. Play the scales and chords as high as comfortably possible.

The jazz player should always be prepared to draw on everything he knows, from any source, concerning scales and chords. He should commit to memory the many scales and chord exercises from such books as Arban, Klosè, Hanon, Czerny, Simandl, *The Universal Method*, and other diverse sources. The jazz player should work diligently toward the acquisition of equal skill and facility in all keys. In all exercises he should vary rhythm, meter, tempo and tessitura.

In order that the practice of the scales and chords may follow some order, observe the following suggestions.

1. Practice scales and chord patterns moving around the key circle (see figure below) in perfect fourths: C-F-Bb-Eb-Ab-Db-Gb-B-E-A-D-G-C. (Start and work clockwise, that is, left to right, back to the point of origination.)

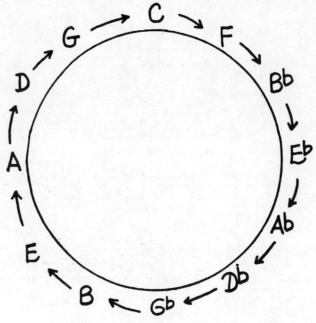

Here is an example of major scales moving around the key circle:

Here is an example of chords moving around the key circle:

2. Practice scales and chord patterns moving in perfect fifths: C-G-D-A-E-B-F#-C#-Ab-Eb-Bb-F-C. Here is an example of scales moving in perfect fifths:

Chords moving in perfect fifths:
- (a) Do the chord exercises in #1 moving in perfect fifths.
- (b) Try the following exercise moving in perfect fifths; then practice all triads and 7th chords in the same manner.

3.  Practice scales and chord patterns moving chromatically up and down: C-C#-D-D#-E-F-F#-G-G#-A-A#-B-C (up) and C-B-Bb-A-Ab-G-Gb-F-E-Eb-D-Db-C (down).

Here is an example of scales moving up chromatically:

Chords moving up chromatically (practice all triads and seventh chords in the same manner):

4.  Scales and chords should be practiced using whole step movement.  There are two different starting points for this exercise, and all scales and chords should be practiced through both sequences: (a) C-D-E-F#-G#-A#-C and (b) F-G-A-B-C#-D#-F.

Here is an example of scales moving up by whole steps using the first sequence:

Here is an example of scales moving up by whole steps using the second sequence:

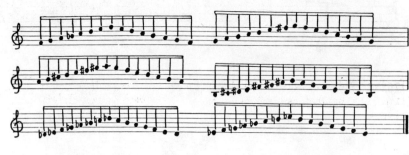

Here is an example of a chord exercise with triads moving up by whole steps using the first sequence:

Practice all triads and seventh chords in the same manner, using both sequences.

5. Scales should be practiced diatonically, in broken thirds, broken fourths, broken fifths, etc., as in the following example:

6. As soon as fluency permits, scales should be practiced starting on each diatonic degree, for example, the C major scale going from C to C, then from D to D, then from E to E, and so forth. The player should practice all types of scales.

Also, as soon as fluency permits, chords should be practiced in all inversions, as in the following example:

On a C major seventh chord the notes would be C-E-G-B, E-G-B-C, G-B-C-E, and B-C-E-G. The player should practice all types of triads in inversions (major, minor, augmented, and diminished) and should also practice all types of seventh, ninth, eleventh, and thirteenth chords in inversions according to his level of development.

Next he should mix the different quality chords and inversions, as in the following example:

Practice all triads and seventh chords in the same manner, as in the following example:

Next the triads should be practiced in the following manner: D minor to G major, C minor to F major, etc., as in example A, or as sevenths in the following manner: Dmi₇ to Do, Cmi₇ to Co, etc., as in example B.

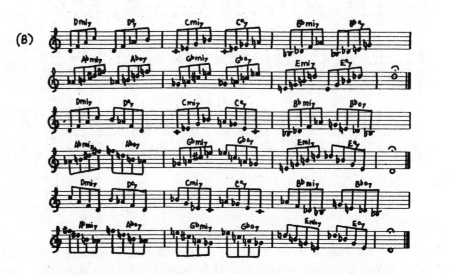

Next the player should practice playing the seventh, ninth, eleventh, and thirteenth chords in the same manner, as in the following example:

All exercises should be practiced in all inversions and mixtures of inversions, for example, a first inversion chord followed by a second inversion chord, followed by a root position chord, etc., as in the following examples:

proper resolution:

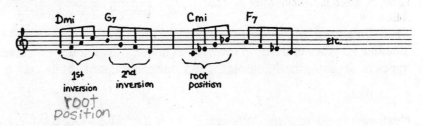

in inversion:

All exercises should be practiced in all keys and using all root movements, as in the following examples:

chromatic:

10

whole step:

cycle:

All exercises should be practiced in all meters, at all tempi, in all registers, at all dynamic levels, in all inversions, in all rhythms, and in every tessitura, some of which are exemplified by the following:

varied rhythm:

varied meter:

## SUGGESTED MATERIALS FOR USE WITH THIS CHAPTER . . .

Jamey Aebersold series: *A New Approach to Jazz Improvisation. Volume 1: A New Approach to Jazz Improvisation. Volume 24: Major & Minor. Volume 26: The Scale Syllabus.*

## SUGGESTED ASSIGNMENTS . . .

1. Practice the exercises on pages 11-16 of *Techniques of Improvisation, volume 2: The II V₇ Progression* by David Baker.

2. Practice major scale exercises or chord exercises from as many different sources as possible.

3. Practice any of the major scale exercises in the first section of *Techniques of Improvisation, volume 1: A Method for Developing Improvisational Technique (Based on the Lydian Chromatic Concept by George Russell)* by David Baker.

# Chapter III

# THE USE OF DRAMATIC DEVICES

All music is drama, and on the ability of the improvisor to handle dramatic devices rests a considerable portion of his success as a jazz player. There is an infinite variety of ways to play a given phrase, a scale, one chord, or even one note. The performer is encouraged to be as adventurous as possible. No combination of scale patterns and dramatic devices should be considered too "far out". The jazz player must work constantly to create and maintain interest using dramatic devices. Working within the following areas, much can be done to create excitement and drama.

1. Dynamics
2. Articulations
3. Range and tessitura
4. Dramatic effects

## Dynamics

Dynamics are varying degrees of softness and loudness which can be used very effectively to create interest in a musical line. Crescendos, diminuendos, plateaued dynamics, and sudden changes in dynamics all contribute to general feelings of excitement. Changes in dynamics help to alleviate staticness in music.

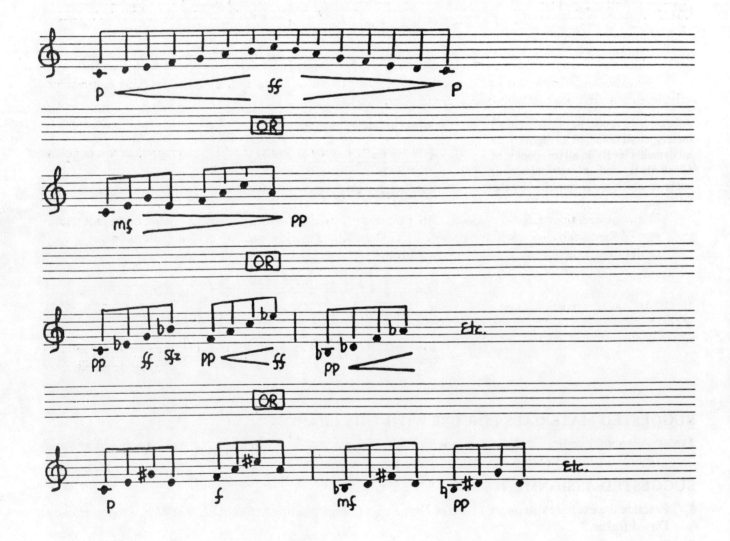

## Articulations

The term articulation refers to the manner in which a note is attacked or a group of notes is attacked or joined together. In any given situation there are a multiplicity of choices available regarding the articulation of a group of notes.

Use these and all other articulations that are a part of your own experience. Draw on other sources for articulation possibilities (method books, solos, exercises, etc.).

## Range and Tessitura

The placement of certain notes or groups of notes in a particular register or rapid changes of groups of notes from one register to another can do much to create dramatic impact in a musical line.

## Dramatic Effects

There are certain musical devices that are traditionally used for dramatic reasons. Some of these devices are a part of the vocabulary of all musical instruments. Others are idiomatic to certain instruments.

In the first category we have such devices as:

1. **Trills** - usually a rapid alternation of two musical tones a degree or half degree apart.

2. **Shakes** - an effect sounding like a trill but with a wider intervallic range.

3. **Mordent** - a trill made by a rapid alternation of a principal tone with a supplementary tone a half step below it.

13

4. **Turn** - a musical figure consisting of four tones the second and fourth of which are the same.

5. **Gruppetto** - a rapid five note turn beginning with the main note.

6. **Appoggiatura** - an ornamental tone preceding another tone.

7. **Glissando** - a sliding effect between two notes.

8. **Portamento** - a slight slide between two notes introduced for expressive purposes.

9. **Rip** - a fast ascending figure (usually executed in a vigorous manner).

10. **Irregular phrases.**

11. **Use of silence.** (Self-explanatory)

12. **Sustained notes.**

14

13. **Repeated notes**.

14. **Extra-musical devices** - shouts, taps, yelps, etc. (Self-explanatory)

15. **Micro-tones** - tones smaller than semi-tones.

16. **Drop off** - a rapidly descending chromatic figure.

17. **Distortions** of tempo and meter. (Self-explanatory)
18. **Variations in vibrato** - speed, width, etc.; lack of vibrato; vibrato placed at the end of the tone.
19. **Changes in the basic sound** of the instrument, physically (throat, airstream) or through outside means (by mutes, etc.).
20. Any **unexpected resolutions**, tonal shifts, etc. (Self-explanatory)
21. **Juxtaposition** of any formerly segregated elements, for example, combining an articulation from one section with a phrasing from another.
22. **Imitation** of the vocal idioms. (Self-explanatory)
23. **Sound intensification**. (Self-explanatory)
24. **Smear** - a very short glissando in which the player approaches the note from slightly below the pitch.
25. **Bend** - a slow mordent.

The second category is best broken into instrument groupings:
1. Valved instruments
2. String instruments
3. Reed instruments
4. Slide instruments
5. Drums
6. Keyboard instruments

## Valved Instruments

1. Devices based on the overtone series.

2. Half valves. 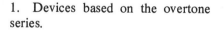 = 2nd valve halfway depressed

3. Alternate fingerings.

4. Different mutings (straight, harmon, cup, bucket, felt hat, wah-wah, etc.).

5. Flutter tonguing.

6. Growls.

7. Double stops.

8. Altissimo playing (extremely high register).

9. Pedal tones.

## String Instruments

1. Mutings. (different mutes)

2. Multiple stops.

3. Different bowings.

4. Pizzicato.

5. Harmonics.

6. Combinations of arco and pizzicato playing.( ⊗ = left hand pizz.)

7. Col legno (with the wood of the bow): battuta (struck with the wood) and gestrichen (drawn with the wood).

8. Sul ponticello (at the bridge).

9. Tremolando (bowed and fingered).

10. Sul tasto (play over the fingerboard).

## Reed Instruments

1. Alternate fingerings. (use alternate fingerings on notes marked with +)

2. Silent fingering (finger the notes, but don't blow into the horn).

3. Sub-tones. (   ) = sub-tone

4. Double stops. Overblow the octave and chords will result.

5. Harmonics (notes above the normal range).

6. Teeth on the reed. (Self-explanatory)

7. Overblowing (extremely loose embouchure).

## Slide Instruments

1. Alternate positions.

2. Devices based on the overtone series.

3. Different mutings (cup, harmon, bucket, straight, felt hat, wah-wah, etc.)

4. Flutter tonguing.

5. Growls.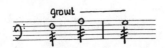

6. Double stops.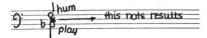

7. Altissimo playing (extremely high register).

8. Pedal tones.

## Drums

Possibilities are too numerous to mention.

## Keyboard Instruments

1. Clusters
2. Unusual ways of playing the instrument, i.e., plucking the strings inside the piano, playing with the fist or forearms, etc.
3. Different uses of pedals
4. Use of prepared piano

   The player should now apply the dramaturgical devices in this chapter to the material in chapter II. Experiment! Make as much music as possible combining the material from chapters II and III.

## SUGGESTED READING . . .

*The Technique of Orchestration* by Kent Kennan. Sections on special effects in each chapter.

*Contemporary Techniques for the Trombone*, volumes 1 and 2 by David Baker. Chapters III, IV, V, VI, XVII, and XVIII.

## SUGGESTED LISTENING . . .

*Porgy and Bess* by Miles Davis (Columbia CL 1274). Miles Davis solos with half-valves, cries, trills, vocal imitations, etc. A virtual compendium of trumpet effects.

*Ascension* by John Coltrane (Impulse 95). Listen particularly to soloists John Coltrane, Pharoah Sanders, and Marion Brown.

*The Jazz Composer's Orchestra* by Michael Mantler (JCOA Records LP 1001/2). "Communications #10" with soloist Roswell Rudd, "Preview" with soloist Pharoah Sanders, and "Communications #11" with soloist Cecil Taylor.

*Live in San Francisco* by Archie Shepp (Impulse A-9162)

*The Empty Foxhole* by Ornette Coleman (Blue Note BLP 4246). "The Empty Foxhole" and "Sound Gravitation."

*Folk and Mystery Stories* by the Charles Tyler Ensemble (Sonet Records Ltd. SNTF-849)

*Nonaah* by Roscoe Mitchell (Nessa N-9/10)

*Free Jazz* by Ornette Coleman (Atlantic 1364)

*Unit Structures* by Cecil Taylor (Blue Note 84237)

## SUGGESTED ASSIGNMENTS . . .

1. Know the four categories of dramatic devices.
2. What is meant by idiomatic devices?
3. List and exemplify some of the dramatic devices common to most instruments.
4. State briefly the reasons for learning about dramaturgical effects.

# Chapter IV

# AN APPROACH TO IMPROVISING ON TUNES

There are three basic tune types found in jazz up through the post-bebop era: (1) vertical tunes, that is, tunes which are essentially concerned with chords or vertical alignments, i.e., "Tune Up" and "Giant Steps," (2) horizontal tunes, that is, compositions which have few chord changes or compositions in which the chord changes move very slowly, i.e., "So What" and "Maiden Voyage," and (3) tunes which are a combination of vertical and horizontal, i.e., "Speak Low," "Dear Old Stockholm," and the blues.

We may approach any composition in a number of ways, three of which follow:

(1) The first approach is a scalar approach where we reduce each chord or series of chords to basic scale colors. This is essentially the direction pointed to in George Russell's *The Lydian Chromatic Concept of Tonal Organization for Improvisation.* In this approach we are less concerned with outlining the particular chords than with presenting a scale or mode that would sound the key area implied by the chords.

(2) In the second approach the player articulates each chord. He might simply use arpeggios and seventh chords in a rhythm of his own choosing or he might use what I have labeled root-oriented patterns such as 1-2-1-2, 1-2-1-2; or 1-2-3-1, 1-2-3-1; or 1-2-3-5, 1-2-3-5; etc.

Using the progression  , this approach would

produce the following example:

(3) The third approach involves the use of patterns either predetermined or spontaneously conceived. This approach is favored by many post-bebop players.

These three approaches are by no means mutually exclusive. In fact, with most players all three are utilized in the course of a single solo. There are many factors which seem to dictate the use of one as opposed to another at any particular time.

If a tune is extremely vertical, some combination of all three seems to work best, according to the player's point of view. If the player wishes to minimize the vertical aspects of the composition, he might do so by using scales. If he wishes to reinforce the vertical aspects he might choose to articulate each chord by using triads, sevenths, ninths, etc. If he chooses to walk a middle ground he might use scales, patterns, and arpeggios.

If a tune is extremely horizontal, the scalar approach seems to be imperative. When the harmony is static (when the changes move slowly), there must be some sort of melodic or rhythmic motion. If we run the chord using arpeggios and seventh chords, the material is too sparse to give the song much forward thrust. The same problems exist if we use root-oriented figurations or II $V_7$ patterns.

If the tune is a combination tune the player might use all three approaches. He might, for example, use II $V_7$ patterns on the changes that last one or two measures, root-oriented patterns on changes that last two beats, and scales on changes that last two measures or more. Many of the finest jazz players use a scheme like the third approach (#3) in some modified form.

# USING THESE APPROACHES ON SAMPLE TUNES

## TUNE I

### I. Vertical Approach

Tune I is essentially vertical but has attributes of both vertical and horizontal tunes. Begin by memorizing the changes; then play the changes using root-oriented patterns. This approach teaches the player to hear roots of chords and provides him a way of marking off the bars of a composition. In the initial stages the player should use essentially eighth notes. In the exercises based on root-oriented patterns we omit the fourth degree of the scale because it breaks down the tonal structure. The player should make as much music as possible by variations of rhythm, transposition of octaves, inversions of chords, repetitions, etc.

The eighth note is the basic unit; therefore, as a general rule, use eighth note figures.

On the major chords simply run the major scale in eighth notes against the chord (C major 7 = C major scale), i.e. the following example:

Also use the patterns on page 11 of *Techniques of Improvisation, volume 2: The II V₇ Progression* by David Baker to enunciate both the II and the V₇ chords (i.e., 1-2-1-2, etc.).

Or use different forms of the major scale, for example triplets, 1-2-3-4, 1-2-3-1, or II V₇, some of which are exemplified in the following:

Or try different forms of the major scale, using broken thirds, 1-3-5-3, etc., as in the following example:

Or use complete seventh chords, as in the following example:

Or use ninth chords, as in the following example:

Use other similar patterns from pages 11-16 of *Techniques of Improvisation, volume 2: The II V₇ Progression* by David Baker.

Or try different inversions of chords, as in the following example:

Or try different resolutions of II to $V_7$, as in the following example:

Or use bebop scales and bebop patterns, as in the following examples:

(A)

(B)

(C)

(D)

All of the foregoing exercises should be practiced varying the meter, tempo, dynamics, register, etc. and adding the excitement devices from Chapter III, as in the following examples:

## II. Horizontal Approach

*Relationship of chords to the major scale.*

Major chords (I) = major scales of the same name, i.e., a C major seventh chord = a C major scale

Minor seventh chords (II) = major scales a whole step below the root of the chord, i.e., a $Dmi_7$ chord = a C major scale

Dominant seventh chords (V) = major scales of the chord of resolution or scales a perfect fourth above the root of the chord, i.e., a $G_7$ chord = a C major scale

Half diminished seventh chords ($\phi$) = major scales one half step above the root of the chord, i.e., a $B\phi_7$ chord = a C major scale

It is important to think in terms of constant modulation; the key signature is not necessarily indicative of the scale areas included in a tune. For example, all II $V_7$ progressions represent different key areas, i.e. the following example:

(1) $Dmi_7$  $G_7$ = C major
(2) $Emi_7$  $A_7$ = D major

*Tune I using scales.*

**Tune I.** In using a horizontal approach to Tune I, which is essentially vertical but has attributes of both vertical and horizontal tunes, try using the major scale to color all chords. For example, in measures 1 and 2 use the C major scale (C major 7 = C major scale, the major scale of the same name as the major chord). In measures 3 and 4 use the Eb major scale, as both $Fmi_7$ and $Bb_7$ belong to the key of Eb ($Fmi_7$ $Bb_7$ is the II $V_7$ progression in the key of Eb).

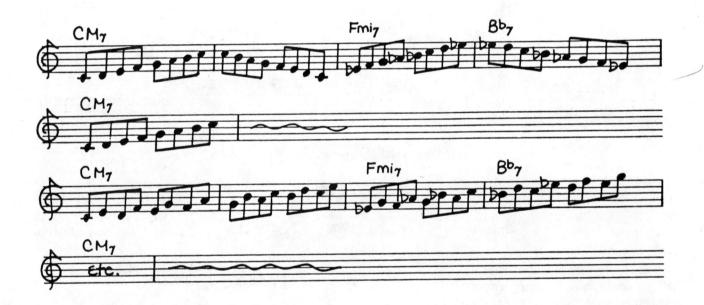

A variation of this major scale approach would be to start the major scales on the name of the chord involved. For example, in using the Eb major scale with the $Fmi_7$ chord, start the Eb major scale on the note F; this results in an F dorian scale, spelled F-G-Ab-Bb-C-D-Eb-F. In using the Eb major scale with the $Bb_7$ chord, start the Eb major scale on the note Bb; this results in a Bb mixolydian scale, spelled Bb-C-D-Eb-F-G-Ab-Bb.

Also try using any of the major scale exercises in *Techniques of Improvisation, volume 1: A Method for Developing Improvisational Technique (Based on the Lydian Chromatic Concept by George Russell)* by David Baker.

### III. Combination Approach

This approach is simply a combination of the first two approaches (vertical and horizontal).

### TUNE II

Tune II is a horizontal composition and demands a scalar treatment. If the player should decide to realize each of the minor seventh chords with a major scale he would have a C major scale for eight measures (Dmi$_7$ chord), an Eb major scale for eight measures (Fmi$_7$ chord), and a D major scale for eight measures (Emi$_7$ chord). Then the player might use any pattern or motif that conforms to a major scale, i.e., "Twinkle Twinkle Little Star" (example A), "In a Country Garden," and "Joy To the World" (example B).

(A)

(B)

Or he might use the kinds of patterns found on pages 1-33 in *Techniques of Improvisation, volume 1: A Method for Developing Improvisational Technique (Based on the Lydian Chromatic Concept by George Russell)* by David Baker, i.e. the following example:

The player might also opt for a combination of major scales and bebop scales, as in the following examples:

This same technique may be employed in dealing with other scale choices such as the diminished scale, as shown in the following examples:

The perceptive player will notice very quickly that despite the scalar approach, chords and arpeggios are still possible and desirable. For instance, the C major scale which colors the Dmi$_7$ chord contains seven different triads, seventh chords, ninth chords, eleventh chords, etc.: C major 7, Dmi$_7$, Emi$_7$, F major 7, G$_7$, Ami$_7$, and Bø. Any one of these chords, when played in a scalar context, will fit against the Dmi$_7$ chord, as in the following example:

# TUNE III

Tune III is a combination of vertical and horizontal aspects. See the following two examples for possible realizations:

## SUGGESTED READING . . .

*Techniques of Improvisation*, volumes 1-4 by David Baker

*Improvisational Patterns: The Bebop Era*, volumes 1-3 by David Baker

*Improvisational Patterns: The Blues* by David Baker

*Improvisational Patterns: Contemporary Patterns* by David Baker

Jamey Aebersold series: *A New Approach to Jazz Improvisation. Volume 1: A New Approach to Jazz Improvisation. Volume 2: Nothin' But Blues. Volume 3: The II V$_7$ I Progression. Volume 16: Turnarounds, Cycles, & II / V$_7$ / Is. Volume 21: Gettin' It Together. Volume 24: Major & Minor. Volume 26: The Scale Syllabus.*

*Improvising Jazz* by Jerry Coker

*The Jazz Idiom* by Jerry Coker

*Patterns for Jazz* by Jerry Coker et al

*The Complete Method for Improvisation* by Jerry Coker

Ramon Ricker Jazz Improvisation series. *Volume 1: The Beginning Improviser. Volume 2: The Developing Improviser. Volume 3: All Blues. Volume 4: II-V-I Progressions.*

## SUGGESTED LISTENING . . .

*Giant Steps* by John Coltrane (Atlantic 1321). Coltrane plays root-oriented patterns on "Giant Steps" and "Countdown," i.e., 1-2-1-2, 1-2-3-5, 1-3-5-3, 1-7-b7-1, etc.

*Kind of Blue* by Miles Davis (Columbia CS 8163). On the horizontal tune "So What" Miles's solo is based on the dorian scale.

Listen to virtually any of your favorite soloists.

# Chapter V

# THE II V₇ PROGRESSION
# AND OTHER WIDELY USED FORMULAE

Although there are an infinite number of ways of combining different quality chords, there are relatively few combinations in widespread use. These combinations we will call formulae. The kinds of formulae enjoying longevity are directly related to style, era, type of tune, tempo, and many other factors.

Just as we have been able to deduce certain seemingly logical chord movements in non-jazz music (for example, $V_7$ usually resolves to I or VI, IV usually goes to II or V, etc.) we can, through the analysis of standards, jazz tunes, etc., extract certain formulae which will greatly aid the jazz player.

One of the most important progressions in music is that of a minor seventh chord resolving up a fourth or down a fifth to a dominant seventh chord. This progression is commonly known as the II $V_7$ progression. An overwhelming portion of the success of the improvisor rests on his ability to handle this progression successfully. Virtually every composition written in the jazz and pop idioms consists of combinations of this most important progression. The following examples show some of the ways of combining II $V_7$ patterns.

(A) Whole steps descending

(B) Whole steps ascending

(C) Half steps descending

(D) Half steps ascending

(E) Movement up or down by regular or irregular intervals

(F) Irregular rate of change

Exercises should be practiced with varied rhythms and articulations, i.e. the following examples:

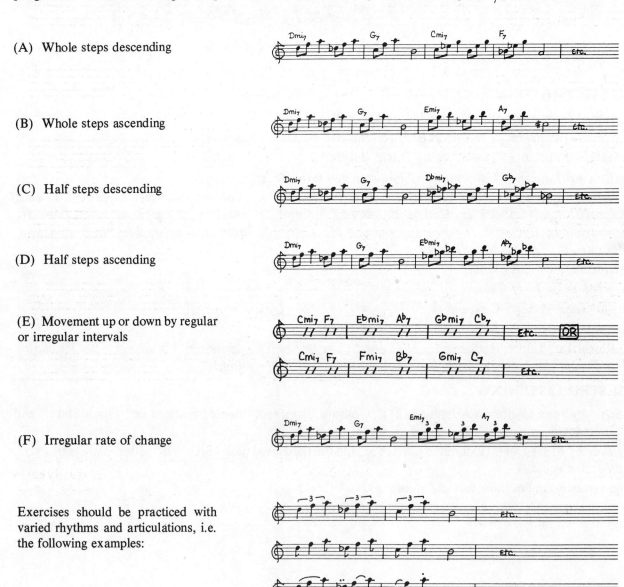

Exercises should also be practiced in varied meters, i.e. the following examples:

Exercises should also be practiced at all tempos from slow to very fast, varying all factors (rhythm, articulation, meter, volume, progression, etc.).

Since a vast majority of tunes use the II $V_7$ progression at a rate of change of one measure apiece, only a few exceptions are listed below. Changes longer than a measure apiece at a moderate tempo usually dictate another approach (scalar, etc.).

In addition to the widely used II $V_7$ formula there are other combinations of chords or chord sequences which have been so frequently used that they now constitute the main body of most popular and jazz compositions. By acquiring facility with these formulae and committing them to memory, the player greatly eases the task of learning to improvise on new tunes. The player will find that few tunes fit neatly into one formula or another, but rather combine two or more of them, often in modified form.

The following formulae are of varying lengths and are all in the key of C. They are to be transposed to all keys and played in all tempi and meters, using all of the dramatic devices.

## FORMULAE STARTING WITH THE I (OR MAJOR) CHORD

# FORMULAE STARTING WITH THE II (OR MINOR SEVENTH) CHORD

# FORMULAE STARTING WITH THE V₇ (OR DOMINANT SEVENTH) CHORD

## SUGGESTED READING . . .

*Techniques of Improvisation. Volume 2: The II V₇ Progression* by David Baker

*Improvisational Patterns: The Bebop Era. Volume 1* by David Baker

*Advanced Improvisation* by David Baker. Volume I, chapter 1.

Jamey Aebersold series: *A New Approach to Jazz Improvisation. Volume 1: A New Approach to Jazz Improvisation. Volume 3: The II V₇ I Progression. Volume 21: Gettin' It Together. Volume 24: Major & Minor.*

*Improvising Jazz* by Jerry Coker

*Patterns for Jazz* by Jerry Coker et al

*The Complete Method for Improvisation* by Jerry Coker

Ramon Ricker Jazz Improvisation series. *Volume 4: II-V₇-I Progressions.*

## SUGGESTED LISTENING . . .

Any recording.

## SUGGESTED ASSIGNMENTS . . .

1. Locate at least five compositions for each of the formulae listed.
2. Find at least ten other formulae currently in use.
3. Identify at least ten examples of combinations of the given formulae.

# Chapter VI

# SCALES AND THEIR RELATIONSHIP TO CHORDS

The following scales and their modes are the most used scales in jazz: major, ascending melodic minor, whole tone, diminished, blues, pentatonic, and, most importantly, the bebop scales.

## THE MAJOR SCALE AND ITS DERIVATIVES

C major 7, 9, 11, 13 (major)

D minor 7, 9, 11, 13 (dorian)

G₇      9, 11, 13 (mixolydian)

Bø    (locrian)

### THE SCALE ABOVE CONTAINS THE FOLLOWING:

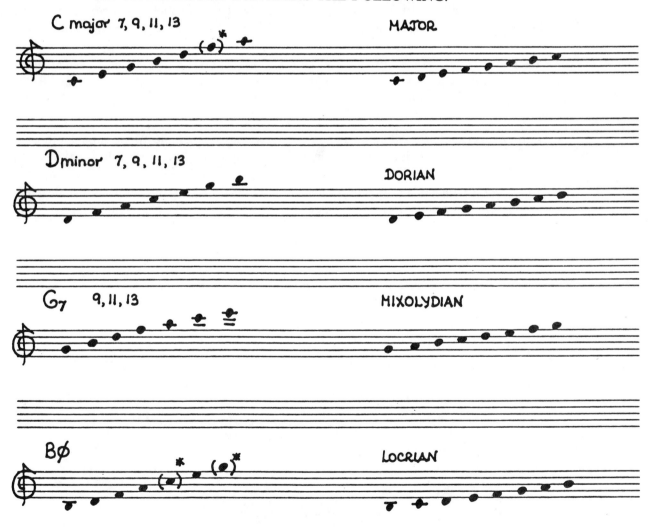

* (   ) the parentheses indicate notes which are usually altered.

In the key of C the chords used in improvisation are C (I), Dmi$_7$ (II), G$_7$ (V), and B$\phi$ (VII). The rules are as follows:

1.  Major chords (I) use the major scale of the same name, i.e., C $\triangle$ = C major scale
2.  Minor chords (II) use the major scale a whole step below or the dorian scale of the same name, i.e., Dmi$_7$ = C major scale or D dorian scale
3.  Dominant chords (V) use the major scale a fourth above or the mixolydian of the same name, i.e., G$_7$ = C major scale or G mixolydian scale
4.  Half diminished chords (VII) ($\phi$, mi$_7^{(b5)}$) use the major scale one half step above or the locrian scale of the same name, i.e., B$\phi$ = C major scale or B locrian scale

Because of the many inconsistencies that exist between theory and performance the major scale is one of the most difficult scales to use and almost always comes replete with admonitions with regard to avoid tones. For example, don't emphasize the perfect fourth of the major scale over a major chord (if the chord is a final chord use a #4 in the scale); over a half diminished chord avoid the tonic of the major scale. The consequence of these traditions and conventions is a complete set of understood approaches to the major scale, including added chromatic tones and other mechanisms that aid in the circumvention of many of these problems; these solutions are dealt with in the section on the bebop scales.

## THE ASCENDING MELODIC MINOR SCALE

The ascending melodic minor scale contains five modes which are among the most important in jazz. The scales/modes and the chords to which they relate are as follows:

1.  Minor chords with a major 7th use the ascending melodic minor scale of the same name as the chord in question, i.e., Cmi $\triangle$ = the C ascending melodic minor scale
2.  Dominant seventh chords with a raised 11th use the ascending melodic minor scale a perfect fifth above the name of the chord in question, i.e., F$_{13}^{(\#11)}$ = the C ascending melodic minor scale
3.  Dominant seventh chords with a raised 9th or a combination of raised 9th and raised 5th use the ascending melodic minor scale a half step above the name of the chord in question, i.e., B$_7^{(\#9)}$ or B$_7$ ( $\begin{smallmatrix}\#9\\\#5\end{smallmatrix}$ ) = the C ascending melodic minor scale

4.  Half diminished chords with a major 9th use the ascending melodic minor scale a minor third above the name of the chord in question, i.e., A$\phi$(Major 9) = the C ascending melodic minor scale
5.  Major chords with a raised 5th and a raised 4th use the ascending melodic minor scale a major sixth above the name of the chord in question, i.e., Eb $\triangle$ $\begin{smallmatrix}\#5\\\#4\end{smallmatrix}$ = the C ascending melodic minor scale

## THE ASCENDING MELODIC MINOR SCALE AND ITS DERIVATIVES

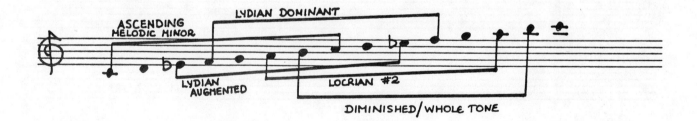

THE SCALE ABOVE CONTAINS THE FOLLOWING:

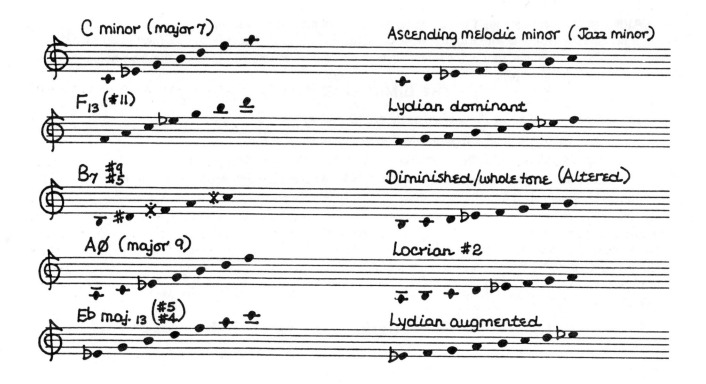

## THE WHOLE TONE SCALE

The characteristics of the whole tone scale are as follows:

1. There are only six different tones in any whole tone scale.
2. All adjacent tones are a whole step apart.
3. There are only major thirds and augmented triads in a whole tone scale.
4. There are only two whole tone scales, and the notes in the two are mutually exclusive.
5. Because of the lack of half steps this scale palls very quickly and must be used judiciously.

$C_7^{\#5}$
$D_7^{\#5}$
$E_7^{\#5}$
$F^{\#}{}_7^{\#5}$
$G^{\#}{}_7^{\#5}$
$A^{\#}{}_7^{\#5}$

} = the C whole tone scale

C whole tone scale

$Db_7^{\#5}$
$Eb_7^{\#5}$
$F_7^{\#5}$
$G_7^{\#5}$
$A_7^{\#5}$
$B_7^{\#5}$

} = the Db whole tone scale

Db whole tone scale

35

Although there are seemingly crucial notes in conflict with those in the minor seventh chord (II), common practice permits the use of the whole tone scale to color the minor chord. The rule is as follows: use the whole tone scale one half step above the root of the minor seventh chord in question, i.e., $Gmi_7$ = the Ab whole tone scale.

## THE DIMINISHED SCALE

The characteristics of the diminished scale are as follows:

1. There are eight different tones in any diminished scale.
2. The diminished scale consists of alternating half steps and whole steps.
3. All possible chord constructs inherent in the scale duplicate themselves at the interval of the minor 3rd, i.e., the following:

$$C_7{}^{\#9}_{b9}{}_{b5} \text{ ----------- appears at ----------- } Eb_7{}^{\#9}_{b9}{}_{b5}$$

$$C \text{ minor}_7 \text{ ----------- appears at ----------- } Eb \text{ minor}_7$$

$$C\phi \text{ ----------- appears at ----------- } Eb\phi$$

$$Co \text{ ----------- appears at ----------- } Ebo$$

4. There are only three possible diminished scales.
5. This scale is one of the most versatile scales.

$$
\left[
\begin{array}{cccc}
C_7{}^{\#9}_{b9}{}_{b5} & Eb_7{}^{\#9}_{b9}{}_{b5} & F^\#_7{}^{\#9}_{b9}{}_{b5} & A_7{}^{\#9}_{b9}{}_{b5} \\
Eo_7 & Go_7 & Bbo_7 & Dbo_7 \\
\hline
\multicolumn{4}{c}{\text{(less specific)}} \\
Gmi_7 & Bbmi_7 & Dbmi_7 & Emi_7 \\
G\phi & Bb\phi & Db\phi & E\phi
\end{array}
\right]
= \text{C-Db-Eb-E-F}^\#\text{-G-A-Bb-C}
$$

RULES: (1) When starting on the root of the seventh chord begin with a half step.

(2) With all other chords, when starting on the root, begin with a whole step.

# THE DIMINISHED SCALE AND ITS DERIVATIVES

Although there are seemingly crucial scale notes in conflict with those in the minor seventh chord (II) and the half diminished chord (VII), common practice permits the use of the diminished scale over either the II or the VII chord. Over the minor seventh, half diminished seventh, or the diminished seventh, when starting the scale on the tonic of the chord, begin the scale with a whole step.

# THE BLUES SCALE

This scale is usually used as a horizontal scale, that is, a scale used to blanket entire areas of a tune as in a blues. The proper scale is determined in two ways: (1) by the key of the music (for example, a blues in F uses an F blues scale, a tune predominantly in the key of F uses an F blues scale, etc.) or (2) the resolving tendencies of two or more chords, i.e., the following example:

could use a C blues scale

C blues scale

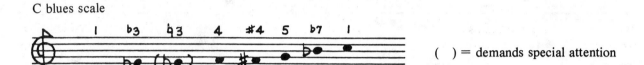

( ) = demands special attention

# THE MAJOR PENTATONIC SCALE

The major pentatonic scale consists of the 1-2-3-5-6 notes of a major scale; using the C major scale as an example, the C major pentatonic scale would be C-D-E-G-A. The major pentatonic scale can be used as either a horizontal scale or a vertical scale. When used as a horizontal scale it is usually used to blanket major key areas. As with the blues scale, the scale of the tonic is usually used, i.e., the following:

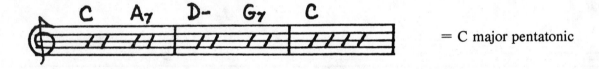

= C major pentatonic

When used as a vertical scale or a scale of high specificity, observe the following rules:

1.  The major chord (I) uses the major pentatonic scale built on the 1, 2, or 5.

C major =
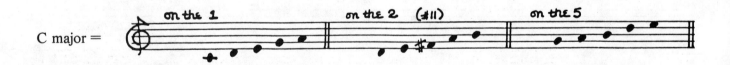

2.  The minor seventh chord (II) uses the major pentatonic scale built on b3, b7, or 4.

D mi₇ =

38

3. The dominant seventh chord ($V_7$) uses the major pentatonic scale built on 1, 4, b7, b3, b5, or b6.

$G_7 =$

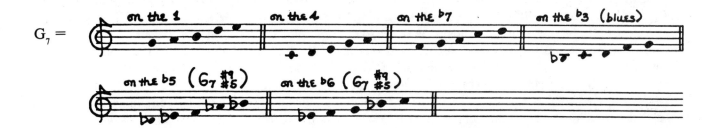

## THE MINOR PENTATONIC SCALE

The minor pentatonic scale consists of the 1-b3-4-5-b7 notes of a major scale; using the C major scale as an example, the C minor pentatonic scale would be C-Eb-F-G-Bb. The minor pentatonic scale can be used as either a horizontal scale or a vertical scale. When used as a horizontal scale, the same rules are observed as for the blues scale.

When used as a vertical scale, observe the following rules:

1. The major chord (I) uses the minor pentatonic scale built on the 6, 7, or 3.

C major =

2. The minor seventh chord (II) uses the minor pentatonic scale built on the 1, 5, or 2.

$D \text{ mi}_7 =$

3. The dominant seventh chord ($V_7$) uses the minor pentatonic scale built on the 6, 2, 5, 1, b3, or 4.

$G_7 =$

# THE BEBOP SCALES (DOMINANT AND MAJOR)

From the early twenties jazz musicians attempted to make their improvised lines flow more smoothly by connecting scales and scale tones through the use of chromatic passing tones. In a detailed analysis of more than 500 solos by the acknowledged giants from Armstrong through Lester Young and Coleman Hawkins, one is aware, first, of the increased use of scales (as opposed to arpeggios and chord outlines) and then the increasing use of chromaticism within these scales. An unusual fact about this increased chromaticism is that, despite the frequent re-occurence of certain licks or patterns, no discernible design with regard to how the extra chromatic tones are added emerges. The overall impression is a somewhat arbitrary or random use of chromaticism.

When one listens to the great players from the distant and near past, one of the main things that tends to "date" their playing (aside from technological improvements in recording techniques, changes with regard to harmonic and rhythmic formulae, etc.) is this lack of unanimity with regard to the use of melodic chromaticism.

From his earliest recordings Charlie Parker can be observed groping for a method for making the modes of the major scale sound less awkward and for rendering them more conducive to swing and forward motion. Gradually, in a systematic and logical way, he began using certain scales with added chromatic tones. Dizzy, approaching the scales from an entirely different direction, began utilizing the same techniques for transforming them. These scales became the backbone of all jazz from bebop to modal music.

A study of a large number of representative solos from the bebop era yields a set of very complex governing rules that have now been internalized and are a part of the language of all good players in the bebop and post-bebop tradition.

Very simply stated, the added chromatic tones make the scales "come out right." Play a descending mixolydian scale and then play the bebop version of the scale and see how much smoother the second scale moves.

There are a number of reasons why the second scale makes more sense. First, in the second scale all of the chord tones are on down beats; and second, the tonic of the scale falls on beat one of each successive measure.

## THE BEBOP DOMINANT SCALE

This scale is spelled 1-2-3-4-5-6-b7- ♮7-1 and the rules governing its use are given with the dominant seventh chord as the point of reference. The scale is also used on the related minor seventh chord (II) and, under special conditions to be discussed later, also on the related half diminished seventh chord (VII), i.e. the following:

$$
\begin{bmatrix}
\text{G-} \\
\text{C}_7 \\
\text{E}\varnothing \text{ (under special conditions)}
\end{bmatrix}
= \text{C-D-E-F-G-A-Bb-B}\natural\text{-C}
$$

RULES:
1. On a dominant seventh chord the scale is reckoned from the root of the chord, i.e., $C_7 = C$ dominant (bebop)
2. On a minor seventh chord the scale is reckoned from the root of the related dominant seventh chord, i.e., G- = C dominant (bebop)
3. When conditions dictate the use of this scale on a half diminished chord its starting point is reckoned from the root of the related dominant seventh chord, i.e., E∅ = C dominant (bebop)
4. The scale usually moves in basic eighth note patterns.
5. In pure form the scale invariably starts on a down beat.
6. In pure form the scale starts on a chord tone (1, 3, 5, or b7) of the dominant seventh chord.

7. Most often the descending form of the scale is used.
8. As long as the scale starts on a chord tone, the line may ascend in a scalar fashion and return the same way.

9. The line may also descend, then ascend in scalar fashion.

10. When the line starts on the 3rd, it may descend chromatically to the 6th, i.e. the following:

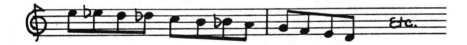

or ascend and then descend chromatically from the 3rd, i.e. the following:

## ENDINGS

The endings of phrases are very important, and two particular endings appear with great frequency:

(1)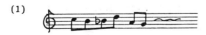

(2)

41

More often than not phrases end on the upbeat of beats one or three, as in the following examples:

(A)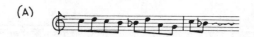

(B)

The line should use whichever of the two endings make this possible. Eventually the player will make this choice intuitively.

Please note that in examples #2 and #A the extra half step between the tonic and b7 has been omitted. The rule governing this situation is as follows: if the line is ending, use a whole step as in examples #2 and #A; if the line is to continue, use the half step as usual, as in the following example:

Practice the different endings starting on other chord tones, as in the following examples:

## STARTING THE SCALE ON NON-CHORD TONES

When starting the scale on a non-chord tone many options exist. Some of the most frequently used ones follow:

1. Use the scale without the extra half step, as in the following examples:

2. Use the scale without the extra half step until you reach the b7, at which time balance is restored and the previous rules are once more operative, as in the following examples:

3. Insert a half step before the first chord tone you come to, as in the following examples:

4. Syncopate the first chord tone you come to, as in the following examples:

42

5. From the b2 approach the tonic from a half step below, as in the following example:

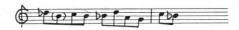

6. From the b3 approach the 3rd from a half step above, as in the following example:

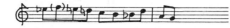

7. From the #4 descend chromatically to the 3rd, as in the following example:

8. From the b6 approach the 5th from a half step below or ascend chromatically to the b7, as in the following examples:

9. When the line starts with a chord tone on an upbeat, all of the preceeding eight non-chord tone rules are operative since it places a non-chord tone on a down beat.

10. Generally, move by step, half step, or skip until a chord tone occurs on a down beat. All of the preceeding examples exemplify this rule.

## EXTENDING THE BEBOP LINE

The bebop dominant scale may be extended through the use of a number of techniques which are a part of the common language of all good jazz musicians. Some of the more common ones follow:

1. Upon arrival on the b7 the line may ascend along a major seventh chord, allowing for extension or change of direction, as in the following examples:

2. Upon arrival on the 3rd, 5th, or b7th, the line may proceed along the outline of the diminished chord containing that note, as in the following example (the diminished chord usually sets up a modulation);

43

Examples A and B may be combined with examples C through H, as in the following example:

3.  The bebop line may be extended through the use of what I shall hereafter refer to as deflection. When leaving the 5th of the scale, the line may be deflected in the manner of the following examples (make sure that when the line resumes its descent the 5th is on a down beat):

4.  The bebop line may be extended by embellishing the root or the 5th of the chord. This is accomplished by delaying the arrival of the chord tone by inserting the notes one half step above and one half step below the tone in question, as in the following examples:

If the line originates from the 3rd or the b7 rule #4 remains operative, as in the following examples:

If the 3rd is to be embellished within a line, start on the b5, as in the following example:

Or skip from the 4th and return by half step, as in the following example:

These techniques for extending lines are particularly useful in modal situations (as in example #I, which follows), in double time passages where more material is needed to fill the same number of measures (as in example #J, which follows), and simply for variety.

44

# ACHIEVING VARIETY WITH THE BEBOP DOMINANT SCALES

1. Start the scale on something other than the first beat of the measure, as in the following examples:

2. Vary the starting note (not just the tonic and not just chord tones), as in the following examples:

3. Vary the endings, as in the following examples:

4. Balance ascending and descending motion, as in the following example:

5. Bury the scale within a line, as in the following examples:

45

6. Turns may be used on any chord tone, as in the following examples:

7. Join bebop scales to other bebop scales, as in the following examples:

8. Join the bebop scales to other scale types, as in the following examples:

9. Use various delays, as in the following examples:

10. Use extensions.

11. Use double time.

## USING THE BEBOP DOMINANT SCALE OVER A HALF DIMINISHED CHORD

When the half diminished chord is treated as a minor seventh (II), then all of the aforementioned rules are operative, as exemplified here:

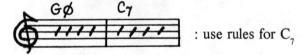 : use rules for $C_7$

However, if the half diminished chord is perceived as part of a II V$_7$ VII situation (i.e., G-| C$_7$| E$\phi$ A$_7$| D- as in "Back Home Again in Indiana," "Whisper Not," etc.), then observe the following rule: treat the $\phi$ (VII) as the related II V progression, as in the following example:

46

# THE BEBOP MAJOR SCALE

The rationale for the use of the bebop major scale is the same as that for the use of the bebop dominant scale. This scale is spelled 1-2-3-4-5-#5-6-7-8 and is used over any major type chord.

RULES:   1.   The scale usually moves in basic eighth note patterns and usually descends.

2.   In pure form the scale invariably starts on a down beat.

3. In pure form the scale starts on a chord tone. For the purposes of the use of this scale the chord tones are 1, 3, 5, and 6, as in the following example:

4. As long as the scale starts on a chord tone, the line may ascend and/or descend in scalar fashion, as in the following examples:

5. When the scale starts on the 9th, descend chromatically to the major 7th, then observe the basic rule, as in the following examples:

6. When the scale starts on the major 7th, descend chromatically to the 5th of the chord, as in the following examples:

7.   When starting on a non-chord tone move by step, half step, or skip until a chord tone (1, 3, 5, or 6) occurs on a down beat.

8. When the solo line starts on a non-chord tone or when the line has a chord tone on an upbeat, insert a half step just before a chord tone to restore balance to the line, as in the following examples:

9. For variety approach the chord tone which initiates the line by a half step above and a half step below, as in the following examples:

47

## ACHIEVING VARIETY WITH THE BEBOP MAJOR SCALE

1. Start the scale on something other than the first beat of the measure.
2. Vary the starting note (not just the tonic and not just chord tones).
3. Balance ascending and descending motion.
4. Bury the scale within less obvious lines.
5. Turns may be used on any chord tone, as in the following examples:

The choices of scales to color chords are not entirely arbitrary but are governed by a number of considerations.

Some of these considerations are:

1. The player's personal taste (one scale sounds better to him than another.)
2. How consonant or dissonant the player would like to be in relation of the chord.
3. Certain alterations in the given chord (**always** choose a scale that takes into consideration alterations in the chord. For example, in a $C_7 \, {}^{\#9}_{\#5}$ [C-E-G#-Bb-D#] choose a dominant seventh scale that includes a G# and a D#.)

The information in this chapter is based on personal observations of many of the most important jazz players of our time. It is beyond the scope of this chapter to deal with the theoretical concepts that underlie the choices of scales that accompany particular chords. Furthermore, this information should not cause the player to close his mind to the many other scale systems and possibilities for constructing and using his own scales.

When dealing with other scale systems it is perhaps better to adopt the nomenclature and rules of that system. However, settle in your own mind which scales are similar and how they operate in the different systems.

## A METHOD FOR GAINING FACILITY WITH THE VARIOUS SCALES

The player is advised to practice all the scales in all keys, at all tempi, in all meters and registers, at all dynamics and using as many dramatic devices as seem appropriate. He is further advised to use the scales whenever possible in an actual playing situation.

In addition to the above I suggest a "total saturation" approach. This approach is just what the title implies, an attempt to exhaust the scale by using it exclusively for an extended period of time in practice. This technique is not unlike John Coltrane's approach to certain modal tunes in which he will choose a scale as his problem and solve it by literally taking the scale apart and examining every implication inherent in its structure, chords, intervals, etc.

The basic rule — make as much music as possible without violating the scale colors you choose.

The player should choose a single chord to improvise on, then choose a scale to color it. Then he should examine the scale charts for all of the possible chords and triads contained in the scale. Next he should examine *Techniques of Improvisation, volume 1: A Method for Developing Improvisational Technique (Based on the Lydian Chromatic Concept by George Russell)* by David Baker for exercises to use on the scale. The following is a sample exercise following this approach:

C₇ chord = the C diminished scale

Now refer to the diminished scale chart for the chords and triads contained in the scale.

Next refer to diminished scale exercises in *Techniques of Improvisation, vol. 1: Developing Improvisational Technique (Based on the Lydian Chromatic Concept by George Russell)* by David Baker.

Play chords and exercises; use your imagination to construct additional exercises, i.e. the following:

The player might decide to concentrate on two chords from the scale, i.e. the following:

Or he might choose one chord and use dramatic devices, tessitura, dynamics, and surprise to make music, i.e. the following:

Or he might decide to use all of the triads in the key plus all of the devices he can muster, i.e. the following:

Or he might take the major and minor triad on C, i.e. the following:

Or he might choose a pattern from the scale book, i.e. the following examples:

Or he might use just a single note, i.e. the following:

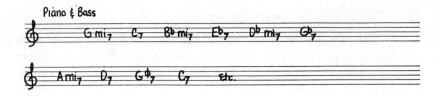

The whole point is to have the player draw on all of his experiences to make music with the material at hand. He is limited only by his own creativity. If the rhythm section (bass and piano) accompanies him, they may play the $C_7$ chord in this case or they may play any of the other chords in the scale. They may play single line counter-melodies or clusters (in the case of the piano) or double stops (in the case of the bass). If the bass player and piano player decide to move outside the pure scale colors, they might play the minor seventh chords and dominant sevenths derived from the scale, i.e. the following:

The rhythm section might play completely free meter, compound meter, in a single meter, free time, or in strict time. Anything goes!

The next step would be to start structuring the solo by:

1. Setting a time length on each chord (i.e. five minutes etc.)
2. Deciding on a set number of bars (eight, sixteen, thirty-two etc.)
3. Deciding a particular tempo and meter.

The techniques of total saturation should be applied to all of the scales in all keys.

The player should then combine changes and scales at random, i.e. the following:

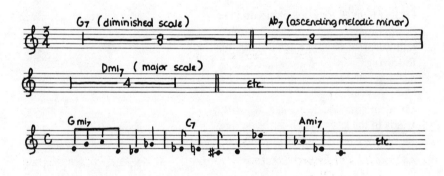

After a very short time, the player should find his technique growing and his facility with scales and chords greatly increased. The next step for the player is to apply this facility and technique to playing on tunes. This grasp of scales should enable him to play "inside" and "outside" on the chord with ease, i.e. the following:

## OTHER SCALE CHOICES

The following chart presents other scale possibilities to color specific chord types. Scales start on the name of the chord unless otherwise indicated.

1. **Major Scale Choices**

| | Scale Name |
|---|---|
| C △ (can be written C) . . . . . . . . . . . . . . . . . . . . | Major (don't emphasize the 4th) |
| C △ +4 . . . . . . . . . . . . . . . . . . . . . . . . . . . . . . | Lydian (major scale with +4) |
| C △ b6 . . . . . . . . . . . . . . . . . . . . . . . . . . . . . . | Harmonic major |
| C △ +5, +4 . . . . . . . . . . . . . . . . . . . . . . . . . . . | Lydian augmented |
| C. . . . . . . . . . . . . . . . . . . . . . . . . . . . . . . . . . . . | Augmented |
| C. . . . . . . . . . . . . . . . . . . . . . . . . . . . . . . . . . . . | Diminished (begin with ½ step) |
| C. . . . . . . . . . . . . . . . . . . . . . . . . . . . . . . . . . . . | Blues scale |
| C. . . . . . . . . . . . . . . . . . . . . . . . . . . . . . . . . . . . | Major pentatonic |
| C. . . . . . . . . . . . . . . . . . . . . . . . . . . . . . . . . . . . | Bebop major |

## 2. Dominant 7th Scale Choices

| | Scale Name |
|---|---|
| C7 .................................... | Dominant seventh (Mixolydian) |
| C7+4 .................................. | Lydian dominant |
| C7b6 .................................. | Hindu |
| C7+ (has #4 & #5) .................. | Whole tone |
| C7b9 (also has #9, #4) ............. | Diminished (begin with ½ step) |
| C7+9 (also has b9, #4, #5) ......... | Diminished/whole tone |
| C7 .................................... | Blues scale |
| C7 .................................... | Major pentatonic |
| C7 .................................... | Bebop dominant |

## 3. Minor Scale Choices

| | Scale Name |
|---|---|
| C– .................................... | Minor (Dorian) |
| C–b6 .................................. | Pure minor |
| C–△ (major seventh) ................. | Ascending melodic minor |
| C– .................................... | Blues scale |
| C– .................................... | Diminished (begin with whole step) |
| C–△ (b6 & major seventh) .......... | Harmonic minor |
| C– .................................... | Phrygian |
| C– .................................... | Minor pentatonic |
| C– .................................... | Bebop dominant starting on F |

## 4. Half Diminished Scale Choices

| | Scale Name |
|---|---|
| Cø .................................... | Half diminished (Locrian) |
| Cø .................................... | Bebop dominant starting on F |
| Cø .................................... | Bebop dominant starting on Ab |
| Cø#2 .................................. | Half diminished #2 (Locrian #2) |

## 5. Diminished Scale Choice

| | Scale Name |
|---|---|
| Co .................................... | Diminished |

## 6. Dominant 7th Suspended 4th

| | Scale Name |
|---|---|
| C7 sus 4 .............................. | Dominant 7th scale, but don't emphasize the 3rd |
| C7 sus 4 .............................. | Major pentatonic starting on Bb |
| C7 sus 4 .............................. | Bebop dominant |

## SUGGESTED READING . . .

*Techniques of Improvisation. Volume 1: A Method for Developing Improvisational Technique (Based on the Lydian Chromatic Concept by George Russell)* by David Baker

*Advanced Improvisation* by David Baker. Volume I, chapter 8; Volume II, chapters 7-14.

*A New Approach to Ear Training for the Jazz Musician* by David Baker

*Ear Training for Jazz Musicians. Volume 3: Seventh Chords/Scales* by David Baker

*The Lydian Chromatic Concept of Tonal Organization for Improvisation* by George Russell

Jamey Aebersold series: *A New Approach to Jazz Improvisation. Volume I: A New Approach to Jazz Improvisation. Volume 2: Nothin' But Blues. Volume 21: Gettin' It Together. Volume 24: Major & Minor. Volume 26: The Scale Syllabus.*

*The Complete Method for Improvisation* by Jerry Coker

*Scales for Jazz Improvisation* by Dan Haerle

*Pentatonic Scales for Jazz Improvisation* by Ramon Ricker

*A Thesaurus of Scales* by Nicholas Slonimsky

*Encyclopedia of Scales* by Don Schaeffer and Charles Colin

*Patterns for Saxophone* by Oliver Nelson

## SUGGESTED LISTENING . . .

Virtually any jazz record with first-class players. For an extensive list of recordings using specific scales see *Advanced Improvisation* by David Baker, volume I, chapter 8.

# Chapter VII

# THE CYCLE

One of the most used root movements in jazz is that of ascending perfect fourths or descending perfect fifths. This root movement underlies the II V₇ I progression.

Following are some exercises to develop skill in using the cycle. Be able to start at any point on the wheel and play back to the point of origination.

③ Review all cycle exercises found in chapter II.

## ALTERED CHORDS IN THE CYCLE

Practice all qualities of 9th chords in the above manner (major, minor, augmented, diminished, half diminished). Alter the 5th, 7th, and 9th.

Practice all qualities of chords in all inversions (9th, 11th, etc.), i.e., the following:

53

Practice all qualities of 13th chords (major, minor, augmented, diminished, and half diminished). Alter the 3rd, 5th, 7th, 9th, 11th, and 13th separately and simultaneously, i.e., the following:

Practice cycles using the patterns in the II V₇ chapter (chapter V), i.e., the following:

Examples of special cycle patterns found in *Techniques of Improvisation, volume 4: Cycles* by David Baker:

For extremely angular effects displace notes by the octaves, i.e., the following:

The cycle is most often found in the form of consecutive dominant seventh chords, i.e., C₇-F₇-Bb₇-Eb₇, etc. It is this form that is most often referred to in jazz language as the "cycle." The root movement of ascending fourths or descending fifths is, however, present in most vertical tunes in the form of II V₇ progressions. The cycle may be used in a multiplicity of playing situations. Some of these are as follows:

I.   Tunes that specifically call for the use of the cycle, i.e., "Jordu" and "Pick Yourself Up."

II.  Tunes in which the cycle might be arbitrarily imposed to make the tune more interesting, i.e., the following examples:

(a) Many standards in the seventh and eighth measures of AABA type tunes (start on the III₇), i.e., the following:

(b) The first four measures of the blues (start on the bII₇), i.e., the following:

(c) "I Got Rhythm" type changes (start on the bVI₇), i.e., the following:

(d) Measures nine through twelve of the blues (start on the III₇), i.e., the following:

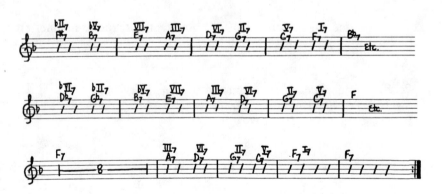

54

(e) Measures eleven and twelve of the blues (start on the III$_7$), i.e., the following:

All cycle exercises should be practiced starting on all degrees of the chromatic scale, in all tempi, all meters, and using all of the dramatic effects in chapter III.

For further examples of the use of the cycle refer to *Techniques of Improvisation, volume 4: Cycles* by David Baker and also to the chart of alternate blues changes in chapter XII, lines 2, 3, 6, 10, 11, 12, etc.

## SUGGESTED LISTENING . . .

*Milestones* by Miles Davis (Columbia CS 9428). "Two Bass Hit": Cannonball Adderley during exchange of fours with John Coltrane

*The Smithsonian Collection of Classic Jazz* (Smithsonian Institution/Division of Performing Arts in association with Columbia Special Products. P6 11891). Side 7. Don Byas solo on "I Got Rhythm," 5th chorus (4th improvised chorus).

*Fat Girl: The Savoy Sessions* by Fats Navarro (Savoy SJL 2216). Fats Navarro solo on "Goin' to Mintons."

Virtually any Thelonius Monk solo on "rhythm" changes.

## SUGGESTED ASSIGNMENTS . . .

1. Be able to play and sing any cycle pattern.
2. Know the places in tunes where the cycle would normally be used.
3. Find at least ten recorded tunes that make use of the cycle.

# Chapter VIII

# TURNBACKS

The term turnback usually refers to a two-measure progression consisting of four chords. This progression serves a number of purposes. First, it helps define the form of a composition. For instance, in a blues the last two measures of each chorus consists of a I chord. The first four measures also consist of a I chord; consequently, the listener hears six measures of a tonic chord. These six measures could be divided $1 + 5$, $5 + 1$, $4 + 2$, $2 + 4$, or $3 + 3$. By using the turnback the performer is able to clearly indicate the correct division $2 + 4$. Secondly, it serves the purpose of providing a link from one chorus to another. A third purpose served is that of preventing staticness. For example, it provides the possibility for harmonic motion where no motion exists. A fourth purpose served is that of providing rhythmic and melodic interest at the ends of sections within compositions.

The performer may introduce one of the turnback patterns when:

1. The composition calls for that specific progression, as in the following example:

2. The last two measures of one section of a tune consists of a tonic chord and the first beat of the next section is also a tonic chord. (The tonic chord may be major or minor.) Here are two examples:

The combination of the turnback with the II V$_7$ progression comprises one of the most important formulae in jazz. The ability to cope with turnbacks makes the improvisor's task infinitely easier.

Virtually every composition written in the jazz and pop idioms can be enlivened and made more interesting by the interjection of well-placed turnbacks. Here are a number of turnback formulae and exercises for realizing them; all exercises are in the key of C and should be transposed to all keys.

## SOME BASIC TURNBACK FORMULAE

These formulae should be realized in a variety of ways, i.e., the following:

1. The manner in which the chords were realized in chapter I (Nomenclature)
2. By referring to materials in *Techniques of Improvisation, volume 3: Turnbacks* by David Baker
3. In the manner of these examples:

Exercises should also be practiced at all tempi from slow to very fast, varying all factors (rhythm, articulation, meter, volume, etc.), as in the following examples:

Exercises should be practiced in various meters, i.e., the following:

Octave displacements are permissible and desirable, as in the following examples:

Exercises from *Techniques of Improvisation, volume 3: Turnbacks* may be combined with exercises from *Techniques of Improvisation, volume 2: The II V₇ Progression,* as in the following examples:

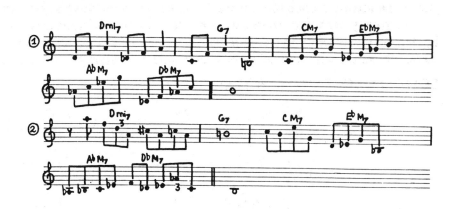

## SUGGESTED LISTENING . . .

*Bird: The Savoy Recordings/Master Takes* (Savoy SJL 220). Miles Davis's solo on "Half Nelson."
*Luminescence!* by Barry Harris (Prestige PR 7498). Slide Hampton's solo on "Dance of the Infidels."

## SUGGESTED ASSIGNMENTS . . .

1. Locate five records that include turnbacks; write down the formulae.
2. Find at least five tunes that contain potential turnbacks within the tune (not as the final two measures).
3. Be able to play at least three different turnback formulae in any key, tempo, or meter.

# Chapter IX

## DEVELOPING A FEEL FOR SWING

1. Listen
2. Imitate
3. Learn bebop tunes
4. Play with a rhythm section

It is my contention that a feeling for the propulsive flow of rhythm that we call swing is best achieved through aural means.

The first step in learning to play notes and phrases in the manner of a jazz player is to listen. The player should make a list of jazz players on his instrument, then go to the record library and listen. Perhaps the initial stages in the listening should be spent in a kind of "bathe in the sound" approach. The player should listen to the "heads" (melodies or compositions) and solos until he can sing along with them. He should then devise syllables that capture the inflections that players use. He should then snap his fingers, tap his foot, nod his head and in general do anything that helps him feel the time in the manner that the soloist does.

Once he is comfortable singing along with records he should then get his instrument and play along with the heads of the tunes, again imitating the players on the record. He should try to imitate nuances, articulations and when possible even the player's personal instrumental sound. (This will start to give him some insights into different approaches to sound and style.) Unless he has an exceptionally well developed ear it will probably be necessary to slow the turntable on the record player from 33⅓ to 16. This change of speed will drop the solo line one octave but leave it reasonably close to the original key. (Some minor adjustments will have to be made in the tuning of the instrument.) Now he must listen and imitate at this slow speed; the notes, articulations, etc. will be more easily heard. Once the notes are learned the original tempo should be observed.

Some additional suggestions:

1. The player should play the "head" with the ensemble, then continue playing the head alone for the next few choruses while the soloists are playing; this will build confidence and a feeling of independence. He should now play the head alone without the record, trying to recall aurally the articulation, nuances, inflections, etc.

2. He should next pick a solo from a record and learn it. He should play the solo along with the soloist, then play it while the next solo is going on, then play it without the record. It goes without saying that if he can find a rhythm section he should then play the tunes and the solos with them. As the player memorizes solos and heads he must try to identify various licks, rhythms, harmonic patterns, and dramatic devices from the other chapters in this book; he should strive to carry the phrasing, articulations, etc. that he learns from the record over into his practicing of similar jazz passages.

3. Once the player has begun to be relatively comfortable with steps one and two, then I recommend learning as many tunes from the bebop era as possible. Why these tunes? Because generally, the lines are eighth-note oriented, teaching the player to think in terms of eighth notes as a basic unit. The tunes are usually built either on the blues or some extremely vertical structure. This gives the perceptive player some notion of the relationships that exist between chords and scales. Most of the melodic, rhythmic, and harmonic vocabulary of today's jazzmen can be easily perceived in these bebop lines (melodies). Most of the lines have been frequently recorded and are also generally found in most fake books. This easy accessibility makes bebop tunes even more valuable. Whenever possible these tunes should be learned directly from the record rather than from a sheet of music. It is not only excellent ear training but it enables the player to imitate the people who should know what is stylistically correct. I recommend learning at least one tune a day. Obviously, in addition to these tunes the player will have to learn ballads, standards and contemporary compositions. In learning these other tunes the same procedures should be followed.

As soon as possible the player should start playing the lines he learns with a rhythm section and other players. He should take solos, listen, analyze, compare, ask questions, imitate, etc.

## SUGGESTED READING . . .

*Listening to Jazz* by Jerry Coker

*The Complete Method for Improvisation* by Jerry Coker

## SUGGESTED LISTENING . . .

Any one of the compositions on the list of 34 essential bebop tunes.

## SUGGESTED ASSIGNMENTS . . .

1. Form a playing group with other instrumentalists and learn bebop tunes.
2. Memorize at least one bebop tune a day.
3. Learn some of Charlie Parker's solos from recordings.

### 34 Essential Bebop Tunes

| | | |
|---|---|---|
| 1. | Anthropology | Dizzy Gillespie |
| 2. | Bebop | Dizzy Gillespie |
| 3. | Bebop Revisited | David Baker |
| 4. | Confirmation | Charlie Parker |
| 5. | Dance of the Infidels | Bud Powell |
| 6. | Dewey Square | Charlie Parker |
| 7. | Dexterity | Charlie Parker |
| 8. | Donna | Jackie McLean |
| 9. | Donna Lee | Charlie Parker |
| 10. | Eternal Triangle | Sonny Stitt |
| 11. | Good Bait | Tadd Dameron |
| 12. | Groovin' High | Dizzy Gillespie |
| 13. | Half Nelson | Miles Davis |
| 14. | Hot House | Tadd Dameron |
| 15. | Joy Spring | Clifford Brown |
| 16. | Little Willie Leaps | Charlie Parker |
| 17. | Mayreh | Horace Silver |
| 18. | Milestones | Miles Davis |
| 19. | Moose the Mooch | Charlie Parker |
| 20. | A Night in Tunisia | Dizzy Gillespie |
| 21. | Ornithology | Charlie Parker |
| 22. | Passport | Charlie Parker |
| 23. | Quicksilver | Horace Silver |
| 24. | Relaxin' at Camarillo | Charlie Parker |
| 25. | Room 608 | Horace Silver |
| 26. | Scrapple from the Apple | Charlie Parker |
| 27. | Serpent's Tooth | Miles Davis |
| 28. | Sippin' at Bells | Miles Davis |
| 29. | Split Kick | Horace Silver |
| 30. | Steeplechase | Charlie Parker |
| 31. | That's Earl Brother | Dizzy Gillespie |
| 32. | Wail | Bud Powell |
| 33. | Woody 'N' You | Dizzy Gillespie |
| 34. | Yardbird Suite | Charlie Parker |

# Chapter X

# DEVELOPING THE EAR

The jazz player encounters some ear training problems that seem to exist only minimally in non-jazz music. The non-jazz player, once the music has been chosen, has the advantage of being able to play a piece of music the same way more than once without stigma. This situation is not the case for the improvising player.

The jazz player must conceive an idea, place it in a tonal perspective, translate it into actual notes for his instrument and play, all this in a split second. This demands a very special kind of hearing — an ability to hear **everything** he plays before he plays it. This is not to say that there are not musical aids for the jazz player. For instance, when a player knows the chords to a tune he may draw on his storehouse of patterns, scales, cliches, etc. and just put the right one in the right place (i.e. on F minor seventh he might use any one of the F minor seventh patterns that he knows).

It is, however, my contention that improvised jazz takes place on three basic levels.

**Level I** — The player plays only things that he has played before; memorized patterns, certain scales which are securely a part of his repertoire, etc. (This is the level of mediocre players.)

**Level II** — The player draws liberally on the patterns, cliches, etc., but he also occasionally tries things that are in his realm of experience but that he has not actually tried before. (This is the level of most jazz players.)

**Level III** — The player consistently plays using ideas that he has not played before, drawing on his fund of knowledge, putting things together that were formerly apart, trying completely different things. (This is the ultimate level to which all jazz players should aspire.)

Needless to say, at advanced levels the ear becomes of paramount importance. The following exercises are designed to develop the player's ear along jazz lines.

1. The player should practice singing and recognizing intervals. He should have someone play intervals for him while he names them. He should name intervals and sing them. The player should play a note on his instrument, then name any other note and sing it.

2. He should extend the interval practice by playing a note, then arbitrarily naming eight or ten other intervals — each interval measured from the last interval.

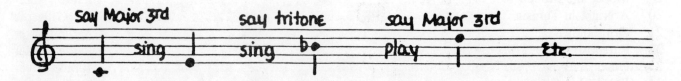

At the end of a given period of time he should play a note on his instrument to check for accuracy.

3. Next the player should practice singing triads of any quality starting on a common tone. (For example, sing Ab. Then, using that as a root, sing major, minor, augmented, and diminished triads.)

4. Next he should do the same exercise using the different quality seventh chords. (For example, sing Ab as the root. Then sing major seventh, minor seventh, diminished seventh, augmented triad, and o seventh chords.)

5. He should now use ninths, elevenths, thirteenths, etc.

6. Next the player should do the triads, sevenths, ninths, elevenths, etc., altering various notes in the chords, i.e., C major$_9$ with a raised 5th, Bbmi$_7^{(+9)}$, C$_{13}^{(+11)}$, etc.

7. Using a single note as the axis the player should sing chords in their inversions.

Sing Ab; then sing the rest of an E major triad.

Now the Ab is the 5th of a Db major triad.

Ab is now the 7th of a Bb₇ chord.

Now the Ab is the 9th of a Gb major chord, etc.

8. Next the player should practice all chords and triads in all inversions, ascending and descending. Examples of ascending versions:

9. Next he should practice recognizing the material in exercises three through ten when somebody else plays them; also name the inversion, etc.

10. He must be able to sing scales of any quality (i.e., major, diminished, whole tone, etc.).

11. The player should sing any quality scale starting on any degree of the scale. For example, sing a major scale starting on the second degree or the sixth degree, etc.

Or sing an ascending melodic minor scale starting on the third, ascending or descending.

Ascending version:

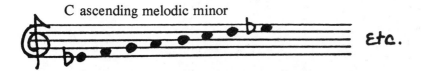

12.  He should sing the diatonic triads, seventh chords, ninth chords, etc. on the various scales, ascending and descending.

Ascending version:

13.  He should sing the diatonic triads, seventh chords, ninth chords, etc. starting from any degree on the scale.

C ascending melodic minor, starting on the 3rd degree:

14.  He must be able to recognize any of the material in exercises eleven through fourteen when played by another person.

15.  He should sing the diatonic seventh chord built on any scale degree.  He should sing all inversions before moving to the next step.

C ascending melodic minor

16.  I recommend that the player devise other similar exercises.

17.  The player should take a bass line off a record, perhaps a blues or other relatively simple tune.

Remember that much of what we accept as evidence of a good ear is merely recognition of things we know, logic, and what is left after the process of elimination has taken place. For instance, in taking a blues in the key of F off the record, we already possess certain facts about the tune and the bass line.

a. It is twelve measures long.

b. The changes are some variation of the following:

$$I_7 \qquad IV_7 \qquad I_7 \qquad V_7 \qquad IV_7 \qquad I_7$$

|| ⊢— 4 —⊣ | ⊢—2—⊣ | ⊢— 2 —⊣ | / / / / | / / / / | ⊢— 2 —⊣ ||

c. It is a probability that measure one starts with the note F; measure five, the note $B^b$; measure seven, the note F; measure nine, the note C; measure ten, the note $B^b$; and the note F on measure eleven.

d. We know some probable scales that the chords come from (if we know the player, we can narrow down the style, etc.).

e. The basic rhythm is probably quarter notes.

All and more of these things we are aware of before we even write or play the first note; consequently, our ear is relieved of a considerable part of its burden. We need only fill in some missing notes and rhythms and verify others. The knowledge gleaned from the chapter on melody construction further aids us by setting up probabilities about how the lines move and where certain notes go (i.e., if the line has just made an ascending skip of a seventh, it will probably turn back in the direction from which it came and resolve by a half step). However, the player should not close his ears to the possibility that something unexpected might take place.

18. The player should move on to more complex bass lines, then to solo lines.

19. Once the player is far enough along to deal with solo lines, I recommend that he dispense with writing the solos down. Instead, he should play and memorize the solos directly from the record. At all times, he should draw on his complete fund of knowledge, using reason and logic to help the ear. (i.e., if he just recognized a D minor seventh chord he should be suspicious that the next chord might be a $G_7$. He should also suspect a II $V_7$ progression before the final chord of the piece, etc.)

20. If possible he should now enlist the aid of another player and play follow the leader. At first he should avoid playing on an actual set of chord changes. He should just play at random and imitate the leader. He should start with brief, closely related phrases and proceed to longer, more complex phrases.

63

21. When the player feels comfortable with number 20, then he should practice his listening technique on a relatively static type of tune: blues, "So What," "Maiden Voyage," etc. Phrases should be chosen that enable the second player to complete the phrase at the same pitch level as the first player. The first and second players should exchange roles frequently.

22. Next the players should proceed to the question and answer type playing where the answer is duplicated but at a different pitch level.

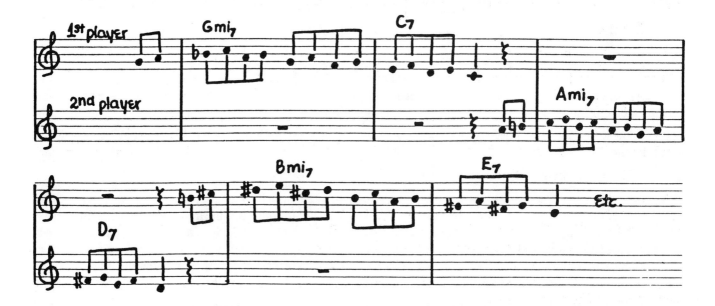

Twenty-two should also proceed from the simple to the complex. As a daily exercise the player might take four or five different tunes in random keys and play through them very slowly without stopping to correct mistakes. He should strive to hear the interval and/or the position of the note in the scale before he plays it. This also applies to hearing any familiar patterns or chord outlines that live within the tune. This pre-hearing has to take place without distorting the tempo. As the player gains confidence he should strive to play each tune at the correct tempo. The player should make sure the keys he chooses for the various tunes are diverse so as to develop equal facility in all keys. If the player has access to a tape recorder, he should record the tunes and play them, making notes of the intervals or chords most frequently missed. He should then strive to improve his hearing and recognition of these intervals or chords.

The next exercise is in the form of a game and is designed to serve a threefold purpose:

a. to improve the hearing;
b. to improve the player's recall;
c. to improve his ability to respond rapidly to musical stimulus.

Two or more players may participate.

**RULES** — The first player plays four or eight measures of a tune (jazz, pop, standard, folk, non-jazz, etc.). The next player has a time limit (15 or 30 seconds) to respond by taking the last two different intervals of the first player's tune and using those two intervals to start another tune. He plays four or eight measures and the next player responds as the second player did.

The player must start with the identical pitches (which means he must develop his sense of relative pitch). As the players become more proficient the exercise can be made more difficult in a number of ways.

1. Use three of four overlapping pitches instead of two.

2. Trim the time limit to five seconds or one or two beats of the previous tune's meter.

3. Restrict the area from which the compositions may be drawn (i.e., only bebop tunes, only show tunes, or only tunes by Thelonious Monk).

I suggest that the player devise other such exercises and use them in a diligent manner. In a brief time the player will have the satisfaction of moving from Level I to Levels II and III.

This entire chapter serves as a suggested assignment.

## SUGGESTED READING . . .

*A New Approach to Ear Training for the Jazz Musician* by David Baker

*Advanced Ear Training for the Jazz Musician* by David Baker

*Ear Training for Jazz Musicians* by David Baker. 5 volumes. 1. Intervals; 2. Triads/Three Note Sets/Four and Five Note Sets; 3. Seventh Chords/Scales; 4. Major Melodies/Turnarounds/I VI$_7$ Formulae; 5. II V$_7$ Patterns.

*Jazz Ear Training* by John La Porta

*Ear Training for Improvisors* by Thom Mason

## SUGGESTED LISTENING . . .

**Listen to your favorite player in an analytical fashion!!!**

# Chapter XI

# THE BLUES

The term "blues" means, to most jazzmen, a twelve measure structure of predetermined form. This form usually contains the $I_7$, $IV_7$, and $V_7$ chords arranged in the following order or some variation thereof:

This basic form is and has been used in one of its modifications by virtually every jazzman, rhythm & blues player, rock & roll player, and country music player since jazz began. Blues still comprise a large part of the modern jazz player's repertoire, so it is an absolute necessity that the jazz player be comfortable with the basic blues changes and their myriad variations.

Because of the unique nature of the blues, this form demands special attention. Although the blues can be treated in any one of three ways (vertical, horizontal, and a combination of the two), it is very often treated as a horizontal tune. One way of approaching the tune horizontally would be to use the blues scale (for our purposes here 1-b3-4-#4-5-b7-1) to realize the whole tune. The proper blues scale is determined by the key of the music, i.e., F blues = the F blues scale. One advantage of the blues scale is that there are no "avoid" tones; all notes fit all chords.

The pentatonic (minor) scale is used in the same manner as the blues scale.

One of the most used of the vertical scales or scales of high specificity is the bebop dominant scale. (See chapter VI: Scales and Their Relationship to Chords.) This scale and all other vertical scales demand a change of scale when the chord changes. The following is an example showing the correct use of the bebop dominant scale on the blues.

The diminished scale is another popular vertical scale often used on the blues, as in the following example:

Likewise, the whole tone scale is often used on the blues, as in the following example:

The modes derived from the ascending melodic minor scale also provide a means for coloring the blues, as in the following examples which use the lydian dominant scale (example A) and the diminished/whole tone scale (example B) respectively:

**EXAMPLE A:  the lydian dominant scale**

**EXAMPLE B:  the diminished/whole tone scale**

In recent years many players have begun using pentatonic scales as scales of high specificity. These scales are usually combined with fourths, as in the following example:

In addition to the use of different scales for variety one might consider restructuring the blues. The first step in the restructuring might be the change to the II $V_7$ progression in measures nine and ten rather than the V chord to the IV chord. Now the player should use all of the knowledge he has concerning II $V_7$ progressions, as in the following example:

The next step toward restructuring might take place in the eleventh and twelfth measures with the inclusion of some form of turnback, i.e., I-bIII$_7$-bVI-bII$_7$ as in the following example:

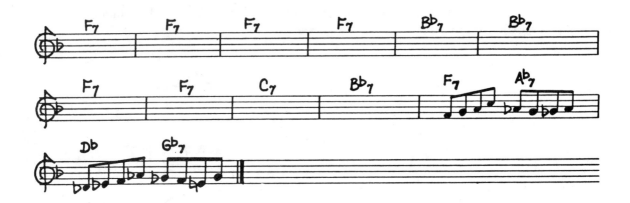

For different harmonic approaches to the blues see "Alternate Blues Changes" at the end of this chapter.
For different material to be used in realizing the blues changes, consult *Improvisational Patterns: The Blues* by David Baker.

## ALTERNATE BLUES CHANGES

All chords in the same column are interchangeable.

Measure numbers are as follows:

| 1 | 2 | 3 | 4 | 5 | 6 | 7 | 8 | 9 | 10 | 11 | 12 |
|---|---|---|---|---|---|---|---|---|---|---|---|
| F7 | F7 | F7 | F7 | Bb7 | Bb7 | F7 | F7 | C7 | Bb7 | F7 | F7 |
| F7 | Bb7 | F7 | Cmi F7 | Bb7 | B°7 | F7 (Cmi7 F7) | D7 (Ami7 D7) | G7 (Dmi7 G7) | C7 (Gmi7 C7) | F7 Bb7 | F7 |
| F7 | Eb7 | Db7 | Cb7 | BbM7 | Bbmi7 Eb7 | Ami7 D7 | Abmi7 Db7 | Gmi7 | C7 | F7 D7 | G7 C7 |
| F7 | G7 | A7 | B7 | BbM7 | Bmi7 E7 | AM7 | Bbmi7 Eb7 | AbM7 | Gmi7 C7 | F7 D7 | Db7 Gb7 |
| F7 | Bb7 | Ami7 Gmi7 | F#mi7 B7 | Bb7 | Bb7 | F7 E7 | Eb7 D7 | Gmi7 | F7 | F7 D7 | Db7 C7 |
| FM7 | Emi7 A7 | Dmi7 G7 | Cmi7 F7 | Bb7 Ab7 | Db E7 | A C7 | F7 | Gmi7 C7 | Dbmi7 Gb7 | F Ab7 | Db Gb7 |
| F F#°7 | Gmi7 Abmi7 | Ami7 D7 | Cmi7 F7 | Bb7 | Ab7 | Gb7 | F7 | Gmi7 C7 | Bbmi7 Eb7 | F7 Ab7 | G7 Gb7 |
| FM7 | EbM7 | DbM7 | CbM7 | Fmi7 | Bb7 | Emi7 A7 | Bbmi7 Ab7 | Dmi7 G7 | Dbmi7 Gb7 | F7 Eb7 | Db7 C7 |
| FM7 | GM7 | AM7 | BM7 | Bb7 | E7 | F Gmi7 | Ami7 Abmi7 | Gmi7 | Gb7 | F Ab | B D |

Measure numbers are as follows:

| 1 | 2 | 3 | 4 | 5 | 6 | 7 | 8 | 9 | 10 | 11 | 12 |
|---|---|---|---|---|---|---|---|---|----|----|----|
| F#7 B7 | E7 A7 | D7 G7 | C7 F7 | Bb7 | A7 | Ab7 | G7 | C7 | Bb7 | F D | B Ab |
| FM7 | Cmi7 Db7 | Gb7 A7 | D F7 | B7 Bb7 | Eb7 Ab7 | Db7 Gb7 | B7 E7 | A7 D7 | G7 C7 | F7 Eb7 | Db7 Gb7 |
| F7 | Eb7 | F7 | Eb7 | BbM7 | Bbmi7 Eb7 | Ami7 D7 | Gmi7 Ab7 | Db E7 | A7 C7 | A7 D7 | G7 C7 |
| F7 | Bb7 | Cmi7 F7 | F#mi7 B7 | Bb7 | Bb7 | F7 Eb7 | Db7 | C7 Db7 | C7 | F7 | Eb7 |
| F7 F#7 | F7 F#7 | F7 F#7 | F7 F#7 | Bb7 B7 | Bb7 B7 | F7 F#7 | F7 F#7 | C7 Db7 | Bb7 B7 | F7 F#7 | F7 |
| FM7 | Emi7 Ebmi7 | Dmi7 Dbmi7 | Cmi7 Bmi7 | BbM7 | Bbmi7 Eb7 | Emi7 A7 | Abmi7 Db7 | Dmi7 G7 | Gmi7 C7 | F7 Bb7 | B7 Gb7 |
| F7 | Ab7 | B7 | D7 | Bb | Db7 Gb7 | F7 | F7 | Dbmi7 | Gb7 | F7 | F7 |
| F7 | D7 | B7 | Ab7 | Bb7 | | | | | | | |

## SUGGESTED READING . . .

*Improvisational Patterns: The Blues* by David Baker
*Charlie Parker Omnibook* edited by Jamey Aebersold

## SUGGESTED PLAY-ALONGS . . .

Jamey Aebersold series: *A New Approach to Jazz Improvisation.* Volume 2: Nothin' But Blues
Blues can also be found on the following volumes of the Jamey Aebersold series:

    volume  1:  A New Approach to Jazz Improvisation
    volume  3:  The II $V_7$ Progression
    volume  6:  All Bird
    volume  7:  Miles Davis
    volume  8:  Sonny Rollins
    volume 10:  David Baker
    volume 11:  Herbie Hancock
    volume 13:  Cannonball Adderley
    volume 14:  Benny Golson
    volume 17:  Horace Silver
    volume 20:  Jimmy Raney
    volume 21:  Gettin' It Together
    volume 27:  John Coltrane

Ramon Ricker Jazz Improvisation Series. Volume 1: Blues in All Keys for All Instruments. Volume 3: All Blues.

## SUGGESTED LISTENING . . .

*Giant Steps* by John Coltrane (Atlantic AT 1311). "Cousin Mary" and "Mr. P.C."
*John Coltrane Plays the Blues* (Atlantic 1382). All tracks.
*Phenix* by Cannonball Adderley (Fantasy F 79004). "Sack O' Woe"
*J. J. in Person* by J. J. Johnson (Columbia CL 1161). "Walkin'," "Misterioso," and "Now's the Time"
*Miles Smiles* by Miles Davis (Columbia CS 9401). "Footprints"
*Kind of Blue* by Miles Davis (Columbia CS 8163). "Freddie the Freeloader" and "Flamenco Sketches"
Virtually any blues record by such giants as Charles Mingus, Milt Jackson, Charlie Parker, Dizzy Gillespie, Horace Silver, Jimmy Smith, Wes Montgomery, et al.

## SUGGESTED ASSIGNMENTS . . .

1.  Learn the basic blues in all keys.
2.  Know as many different sets of blues changes as possible.
3.  Listen to and play with your favorite blues players.
4.  Gain facility with the blues patterns that are a part of the vocabulary of all jazz players. (Use *Improvisational Patterns: The Blues* by David Baker.)

# Chapter XII

# CONSTRUCTING A MELODY

All jazz players must at some point in their careers (preferably early) come to grips with the construction of melodies. The term construction or composition is not used here in the formal sense of writing something down, but rather in a sense consistent with the notion that all improvisation is composition or recomposition.

The tenets of good melody vary with the circumstances, but traditionally there are certain ones we can list:

1. First there must be a proper balance of diatonic movement and skips. Stepwise motion is the general rule in melodic construction. To this we add skips for variety. There is considerable deviation from this rule in the playing of many members of the avant garde, among them Don Cherry, Don Ellis, and Eric Dolphy, to list just a few.

Generally, leaps, except along the outline of the chord, turn back in the direction of the skip. However, if the second note of a skip is the final note of a phrase or is followed by a prolonged rest, the melody may continue in the same direction.

The following is a fairly well-balanced melody. Notice the skips along the chord in measures eleven and twelve; also note that in measures seven and eight the return is in the direction of the skip. Various aspects of this melody will serve to exemplify points of discussion in both this chapter and chapter XIII: "Techniques to be Used in Developing a Melody," so be prepared to refer back to it frequently.

2. The melody should aim in a general manner toward a climax point. All melodies usually have a single climax point or area. This point might be at the highest pitch or in an area in which the general tessitura is high. The main thrust of a good melody is to approach and leave this point or series of points in an effective manner. This might mean, as far as the jazz player is concerned, a gradual buildup over a number of choruses aiming toward a peak. This gradual buildup might be accomplished by means of a series of plateaus distributed over a part of the solo until the peak is reached. Once the climax is achieved, the soloist will usually descend gradually to a point of less intensity. More often than not the lessening of tension and return to normal is much more rapid than the buildup or ascent. In the sample melody the climax is in measure six, halfway through, and the descent is about half the tune.

3. There must always be contrast and interplay between (1) density and lack of density, (2) tension and relaxation, and (3) intensity and lack of intensity. For example, a good soloist will not play in one tessitura for the entire solo or in double time the entire solo because there is not sufficient contrast. The following example shows how a good soloist might plan a solo of four choruses to achieve contrast and interplay:

| CHORUS #1 | CHORUS #2 | CHORUS #3 | CHORUS #4 |
|---|---|---|---|
| single time | some double time | double time | single time to half time |
| medium range | medium range | high range | medium to low range |
| pp | mf | ff | mf |
| thin texture | more involved | dense | lessening of density |

4. In most good melodies there is considerable evidence of repetition which, when combined with other things, acts as a unifying factor. However, the player is cautioned to avoid too much repetition of a curve, a note or a phrase except for special effect. Repetition in the melody can, however, be sufficiently disguised to allow a more extensive use. The changes which effect the disguise might include alteration of intervals, rhythm, dynamics, etc. In the sample melody measures 2, 3, 5, 11, and 12 are modifications of the same curve.

5. Another general rule to be observed: move when the harmonic rhythm is static and relax when there is plenty of motion in the harmonic rhythm. The extremely rhythmic player opens up more possibilities for the rhythm section to engage him in interplay, as in the following example:

6. Most melodies have some unique feature that distinguish them from other melodies of the same type. The melody might contain a sudden rhythmic shift, a note that sounds wrong, a particular interval that is used more than others or some other such device. In the sample melody the main unifying factor is the use of alternating half steps and whole steps (diminished scale order) and the implied major triads in measures 1, 7, 8, 10, 11, and 12.

7. The player must strive for proper balance between the new and the old (the novel and the familiar). Every melody must have enough recognizable elements to provide stability but enough of the novel to prevent the listener from anticipating every melodic, harmonic, and rhythmic occurence.

8. Melodic phrases are not all of the same length; length is by and large governed by the idea itself. Long phrases are usually broken into smaller units with implied cadence points. From a practical standpoint shorter melodies are more easily remembered when it is time to develop them. In the sample melody the first phrase is four measures long and dovetails into the second phrase, which consists of measures five and six. The third phrase is made up of measures seven through twelve.

The preceeding rules are not meant to imply that the improvisor is always left completely on his own to make melodies. In fact, most of the time he has the option of either using the melodic material from the tune he is playing or using other material as a starting point. (Refer to chapter XI.)

The ability to consistently conceive memorable, original melodies is truly a gift, but the methods for constructing fluent, workable lines can be learned.

## SUGGESTED READING . . .

*A Composer's World* (Chapter 4) by Paul Hindemith
*Serial Composition* (Chapter 5) by Reginald Smith Brindle
*Studies in Counterpoint* (Introduction, Chapters I, II) by Ernst Křenek
*The Rhythmic Structure of Music* by Cooper & Meyer
*Structure and Style* (Section I) by Leon Stein

## SUGGESTED RECORDINGS . . .

Listen to any recordings of performers you enjoy. Pay particular attention to the points raised in this chapter.

## SUGGESTED ASSIGNMENTS . . .

1. Study some of your favorite composed melodies with regard to the rules listed in this chapter.
2. Transcribe and study improvised solos by your favorite players. See how they adhere or do not adhere to the tenets espoused in this chapter.
3. Practice improvising, concentrating on one of the rules at a time. As fluency increases, include other rules.

# Chapter XIII

# TECHNIQUES TO BE USED IN DEVELOPING A MELODY

We will now examine some of the techniques used to develop a melody. Again the over-riding consideration is the use of tension and relaxation.

## REPETITION

Repetition is an important unifying principle used in traditional western music (jazz included). Exact repetition palls very quickly so the task of the player is to use repetition skillfully and subtly. Exact repetition of an idea more than two times, except for special purposes, is rarely effective.

1. One of the easiest techniques for avoiding exact repetition is octave displacement of all or part of a line. Its strength and its weakness is its lack of subtlety.

OR

2. Another technique for avoiding exact repetition is sequence. Sequence is the technique of transposing a section of a theme by an interval other than an octave. This usually implies a change of key center and for this reason it proves valuable to the jazz player who is faced with the concept of constant modulation in dealing with vertical structures (changes). Even sections using this technique become uncomfortable to listen to after two or three repetitions.

The technique is considerably more effective if slight changes are made in the sequences, as in the following examples:

(a) Change of contour

(b) Harmonic changes

(c) Rhythmic changes

(d) Altered notes

3. **Extension** is a technique of modification in which the phrase is extended to include more measures than its original form. The process might take place over many measures with a note or notes being added to each subsequent repetition. This technique is particularly effective in a situation where the harmony is slow-moving or static, as in "So What," "Speak Low," the blues, etc. (Needless to say, this technique presupposes the ability of a player to remember the phrases he plays.)

Extension:

4. **Truncation** is the technique of omitting a note or notes from the end of a musical phrase. As with extension, the process may take place over an extended period of time, and as with extension, the technique is particularly effective in a situation where the harmony is slow-moving or static.

Truncation:

Both extension and truncation are more effective when the phrases which utilize the techniques are consecutive; however, the technique is still useful as long as the phrases are close together enough to be remembered and perceived as modifications of the same basic idea. Thelonious Monk's "Straight No Chaser" is a marvelous example of both extension and truncation.

5. **Augmentation** (or elongation) refers to the process of increasing the rhythmic values of a theme. This is usually done by increasing the value of the notes by a constant ratio. A caution: don't stretch the theme too much; it loses its identity.

Augmentation:

6. **Diminution** is the process of decreasing the rhythmic values of a theme. This is usually done by decreasing the value of the notes by a constant ratio.

Diminution:

In an actual jazz situation augmentation and diminution are rarely used in a pure form and are generally used briefly, are modified, and are used in combination with each other and other developmental techniques.

7. **Fragmentation** is the technique of presenting the theme in parts. This particular technique is very popular with many jazz players, among them Thelonious Monk, J. J. Johnson, and John Lewis, to name just a few. Almost all jazz players use this technique, consciously or otherwise.

Fragmentation:   (The material in this example comes from the sample melody in chapter XII.)

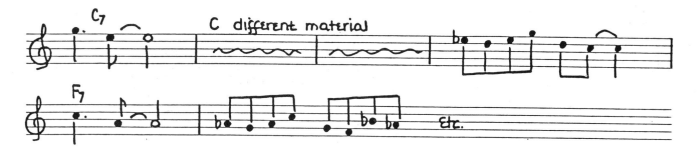

**8. Inversion. 9. Retrograde. 10. Retrograde inversion.**

All motifs or themes have four basic forms: original, inversion, retrograde, and retrograde inversion.

8. **Inversion** changes each ascending interval into the corresponding descending interval and vice versa.

Inversion: (This example is an inversion of the first three measures of the sample melody from chapter XII.)

9. **Retrograde** is the playing of a theme backwards, that is, beginning with the last note and ending with the first note.

Retrograde: (This example is the retrograde of the first four measures of the sample melody from chapter XII.)

10. **Retrograde inversion** is the technique of combining retrograde and inversion, that is, playing a line both upside down and backwards.

Retrograde inversion: (This example is the retrograde inversion of a portion of the first four measures of the sample melody from chapter XII. The example starts at measure four, as does the example of retrograde, and moves backwards towards measure one.)

Inversion, retrograde, and retrograde inversion are not generally considered practical or musically feasible for use in a jazz context except in extremely modified form. These strictly calculated practices are the antithesis of jazz. First of all, it would require a remarkably mathematical mind to remember and transform any but the simplest themes exactly; once transformed they would probably appeal only to the pendant. Usually a musical hint of one or more of the three techniques is enough to convey the basic idea.

11. **Rhythmic and melodic displacement** are techniques of removing a rhythm or a theme from its usual position in the time or harmony. The following examples use material from the sample melody in chapter XII:

OR

12. **Contextual placement for consonance or dissonance** is a technique of placing a theme or section of a theme within the harmony in such a manner as to render the theme consonant or dissonant by context. In most cases the theme remains unaltered. The following example uses material from the sample melody in chapter XII:

13. **Tonal shift** refers to the technique of arbitrarily moving a theme or theme fragment to another key area irrespective of the underlying harmony. This is a technique practiced more and more by modern players to add harmonic and melodic interest to the line. It usually occurs with the horn moving independently of the rhythm section and often involves a half step or whole step movement. (Listen to Sonny Rollins, Ornette Coleman, and John Coltrane.) The following example uses material from the sample melody in chapter XII:

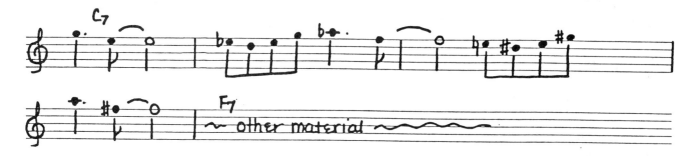

14. **Change of mode** is simply the technique of changing the scale color of the theme or theme fragments, for example, changing from the major scale color to the ascending melodic minor scale color. In the following example which uses material from the sample melody in chapter XII, the diminished scale color in measures five and six has been changed to a major scale color:

15. **Juxtaposition of tune sections** is the process of using the material from one section of the tune in another section of the tune (either verbatim or altered). In the following example which uses material from the sample melody in chapter XII, transposed material from measures nine and ten is used in measures one and two:

16. **Simplifying or complicating the line.** Simplification takes place when we **remove** everything but the essence of the line, getting rid of embellishing and decorating material. Complication takes place when we **add** embellishing and decorative (or other additional) material to the line. The following examples use material from the sample melody in chapter XII.

Simplification:

Complication:

17. **Alteration of shape.** This can be done in two ways: (1) changing the size of the interval and (2) changing the contour of the line. The following examples use material from the sample melody in chapter XII.

Changing the size of the interval:

Changing the contour of the line:

18. **Combining elements of the composition at random** simply means joining measures together that were formerly segregated. The following example uses material from the sample melody in chapter XII:

19. Isolating and using rhythmic aspects of the composition, for instance, using unique rhythmic factors. The following example uses material from the sample melody in chapter XII:

**SUGGESTED READING . . .**

*Serial Composition* (chapters 14 and 15) by R. S. Brindle

*Techniques of Twentieth Century Composition* (chapters 12 and 13) by Leon Dallin

*Jazz: An Introduction to Its Musical Basis* (chapter 2) by Avril Dankworth

*Advanced Improvisation* (chapter 15) by David Baker

**SUGGESTED LISTENING . . .**

Play records of your favorite players. Identify the various techniques described in this chapter.

**SUGGESTED ASSIGNMENTS . . .**

1. Locate and write down in a notebook for future reference examples from recordings of each of the techniques described in this chapter.

2. In jam sessions try the techniques described in this chapter.

# Chapter XIV

# CONSTRUCTING A JAZZ CHORUS

Before the player plays the first note of a jazz chorus there are certain decisions he must make.
1. Determine in which style the tune is to be played. (i.e., bebop, free, swing, etc.)
2. Approximate length of the chorus.
3. Type of rhythm section with which he'll be playing.
4. What went before (instant decision).
5. How to relate to the rhythm section.
6. Source of basic melodic material.

1. Too often the jazz musician gives little thought to playing a composition in a manner that is stylistically authentic. This does not mean that he needs to imitate or be unoriginal but rather that he should operate his creativity within the circumscribed stylistic and musical area of the particular composition. Each composition brings its own set of problems and the success or failure of the player depends on his ability to solve these problems. Few things are more disconcerting than hearing a player in a bebop session (changes prevailing) playing in a free manner. By the same token, one should not rely on "change running" to realize a tune by Ornette Coleman. The player should be conscious of the fact that all art is concerned with problem solving. He must first ascertain the nature of the problem, then set about determining the best way to solve it.

2. As closely as possible the player should try to ascertain in a general manner the length that his chorus will be. It better equips him to pace himself musically and physically. It also allows him to use his material more intelligently and economically.

3. Very quickly the player should "size up" the rhythm section and make whatever adjustments are necessary. For example, if the rhythm section is given to high-tension playing with great volume then the player must respond in a manner compatible with this set of circumstances.

4. Some decisions about the material to be used can be made while the preceding soloist is playing but other decisions must be made at the instant when the new soloist starts. The player must decide whether to continue in his predecessor's manner (harmonically, melodically, rhythmically, etc.) or to start a new attack, with different material and change of mood.

5. How to relate to the rhythm section is a matter of great concern and one that must be solved time and time again in the course of a solo. It seems that there are three basic ways to relate to and play with a rhythm section.

a. Playing **with** the rhythm section. (i.e., moving tonally, moving rhythmically, double timing when the rhythm double times, etc.)

b. Playing against — contrasting the volume, the density, the registers of the rhythm section, not double timing when the rhythm section does, double timing when the rhythm section plays straight or half time, etc.

c. Playing on a parallel plane using the same material (or various aspects of it) as the rhythm section but functioning relatively independently.

Obviously there is a great deal of overlapping between the three categories and most players do all three, many times within the same chorus.

6. Where does the player go for material to be used in his solo? There are a number of sources, some of which are:

a. The tune itself (rhythmic, harmonic or melodic aspects). The player must make value judgments about the worth of the tune, its accessibility, etc. He must decide for himself whether to try to use it and then what aspect of it to use. Here the player is advised to try to use some unique element of the composition.

b. Something that suggests the mood of the tune. (Pretty, slow, angular, etc.)

c. Material from outside the tune. This includes other similar compositions, tunes from the same show (if a show tune), quotes, ad infinitum.

d. "Licks," "cliches," "patterns," etc.

The general format of a jazz chorus will vary from soloist to soloist and from tune to tune. Some jazzmen favor working from the simple to the complex. (Wes Montgomery's favorite format was single lines, followed by octaves, then followed by chords.) Others prefer to start with simple ideas, move to complex ideas, and then return to simple ideas. Still others will start at a peak and stay there (Coltrane, Miles, etc.). Most players use all of the techniques according to the situation.

As we move from the bebop into the avant garde we find more and more the change from basically developmental forms to additive forms. The player is encouraged to listen to many players of all persuasions and then find his own way.

One more general rule: **Economize** — Don't use all you know in every chorus, the listener can only absorb about two new ideas per chorus.

## SUGGESTED READING . . .

*Jazz Pedagogy* (chapter VII) by David Baker

*Listening to Jazz* by Jerry Coker

*The Complete Method for Improvisation* by Jerry Coker

Jamey Aebersold Play-Along Series: *A New Approach to Jazz Improvisation. Volume 21: Gettin' It Together.*

*The Giants of Jazz* series by David Baker (books of transcriptions). Includes volumes on Miles Davis, John Coltrane, Cannonball Adderley, Sonny Rollins, Fats Navarro, and Clifford Brown.

*The David Baker Jazz Monograph Series* (books of transcriptions). Includes volumes on Charlie Parker and J.J. Johnson.

## SUGGESTED LISTENING . . .

*Milestones* by Miles Davis (Columbia CS 9428). "Straight No Chaser," all soloists.

*The Shape of Jazz to Come* by Ornette Coleman (Atlantic 1317). Ornette Coleman's solo on "Peace."

*Miles Smiles* by Miles Davis (Columbia CL 2601). "Freedom Jazz Dance," all soloists.

*Outstanding Jazz Compositions of the Twentieth Century* (Columbia C2S 831). Bill Evan's solo on "All About Rosie."

Virtually any solo by such jazz giants as Wes Montgomery, Thelonious Monk, Sonny Rollins, John Lewis, J.J. Johnson, and Charlie Parker.

## SUGGESTED ASSIGNMENTS . . .

1. Know the six considerations before starting a chorus.
2. Name at least one criterion for determining the success of a jazz chorus.
3. Analyze the playing of your favorite players with respect to their approaches to format.
4. Know some sources for thematic material.

# Chapter XV

# CHORD SUBSTITUTIONS

Very often the jazz player will find it advisable to use a different set of chords than those suggested by a piece of sheet music or a recording. There can be many reasons for making such a decision, among them the following:

1. To relieve the monotony of endless repetitions of the same chord changes
2. To introduce tension into an otherwise static situation
3. To provide a better (stronger) bass line
4. To provide more challenging and interesting vertical structures on which to improvise
5. To make a tune easier or more difficult to play on
6. To change the harmonic texture, for example, simple to complex and vice versa

Sometimes the technique may involve nothing more than re-interpreting the given chords (as in example A), or consolidating changes (as in example B), or some other simple task.

Example A:  Dmi₆  E₇  is really  Bø₇  E₇

Example B:  C₇ C₁₃ C₁₁ C₇(♭9)  when consolidated equals  C₇

At other times the technique may involve a much more complex reordering that may change the entire thrust of a set of chords.

**Non-contextual Substitutions**

Non-contextual substitutions are substitutions that seem to work relatively independently of the musical context. Obviously, it is not possible to operate in a musical manner without considering the harmonic surroundings to some degree.

**Major Chords (I): Non-contextual substitution possibilities**

1. For the major chord substitute the minor seventh chord a minor third below the root of the chord, as in the following example:

CM₇ CM₆ = Ami₉ (vi)

2. For the major chord substitute the minor seventh chord a major third above the root of the chord, as in the following example:

CM₇ CM₆ = Emi₇ (III)

3. For the major chord substitute the dominant seventh with a raised eleventh a perfect fourth above the root of the chord, as in the following example:

CM₇ CM₆ = F₇(+11)(IV)

84

4. For the major chord substitute any other major chord.

## Minor Chords (II): Non-contextual substitution possibilities

1. For the minor chord substitute its dominant seventh, the root of which will be a perfect fourth above the root of the minor seventh chord, as in the following example:

2. For the minor chord substitute the major chord a minor third above the root of the chord, as in the following example:

3. For the minor chord substitute the half diminished seventh chord a minor third below the root of the chord, as in the following example:

4. For the minor chord substitute the other minor seventh chords which have their roots in the same diminished chord and their accompanying resolutions, as in the following examples:

Dmi$_7$, Fmi$_7$, Abmi$_7$, and Bmi$_7$ all have their roots in the same diminished chord; therefore, the following substitutions for Dmi$_7$ are possible according to the preceding rule.

5. For the minor chord substitute the diminished chord of the same name as the minor seventh chord in question, as in the following example (you can also use any of the inversions of the diminished chord):

6. For the minor chord substitute any other minor seventh type chord.

7. For the minor chord substitute any dominant seventh type chord.

8. For the minor chord substitute any diminished type chord.

9. For the minor chord substitute any half diminished seventh chord (minor seventh with a flat 5).

85

## Dominant Seventh Chords (V): Non-contextual substitution possibilities

1. For the dominant seventh chord substitute the minor seventh a perfect fourth below the root of the chord, as in the following example:

2. For the dominant seventh chord substitute the major chord a whole step below the root of the chord, as in the following example:

3. For the dominant seventh chord substitute the half diminished seventh chord a major third above the root of the chord, as in the following example:

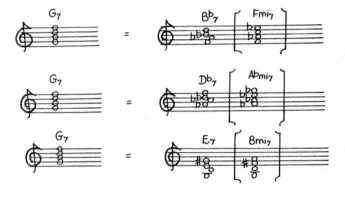

4. For the dominant seventh chord substitute the other dominant seventh chords which have their roots in the same diminished chord and their accompanying minor seventh chords, as in the following examples:

$G_7$, $Bb_7$, $Db_7$, and $E_7$ all have their roots in the same diminished chord; therefore, the following substitutions for $G_7$ are possible according to the preceding rule.

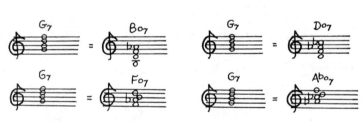

5. For the dominant seventh chord substitute the diminished chord a major third above the root of the chord, as in the following example (you can also use any of the inversions of the diminished chord):

6. For the dominant seventh chord substitute any other dominant seventh chord.

7. For the dominant seventh chord substitute any minor seventh chord.

8. For the dominant seventh chord substitute any diminished seventh chord.

9. For the dominant seventh chord substitute any half diminished seventh chord (minor seventh with a flat 5).

### Contextual Substitutions

Contextual substitutions are substitutions which work only in specific contexts. In contextual substitutions a like or similar chord progression is presupposed if one is to use the substitutions given in the examples which follow. Additional examples of contextual substitutions can be found in chapter XI: The Blues, in the chart entitled "Alternate Blues Changes."

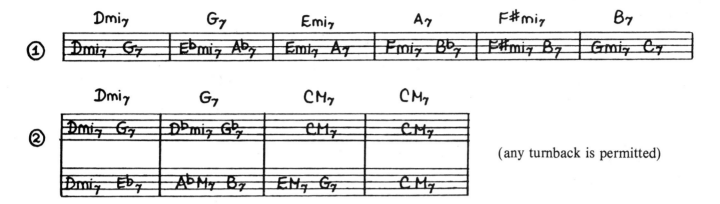

The bottom line of example #2 is a set of changes known as the Coltrane changes. As can be readily discerned we can use these changes over a II/V₇/I progression that covers four measures, as in the following example:

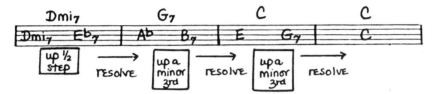

Note that the second chord (on beat three) of each measure is a dominant seventh which resolves to a major chord on beat one of measures 2, 3, and 4.

Example #3 is a chart illustrating a matrix which I evolved and developed based on the Coltrane changes.

| Dmi7 | G7 | C | C |
|---|---|---|---|
| Dmi7    Eb7 | Ab    B7 | E    G7 | C |
| Dmi7    Bbmi7 Eb7 | Ab    F#mi7 B7 | E    Dmi7 G7 | C |
| Dmi7 G7    Bbmi7 Eb7 | Ab Fmi7    F#mi7 B7 | E C#mi7    Dmi7 G7 | C |
| Fmi7 | Bb7 | Eb | Eb |
| Fmi7    Gb7 | B    D7 | G    Bb7 | Eb |
| Fmi7    Dbmi7 Gb7 | B    Ami7 D7 | G    Fmi7 Bb7 | Eb |
| Fmi7 Bb7    Dbmi7 Gb7 | B G#mi7    Ami7 D7 | G Emi7    Fmi7 Bb7 | Eb |
| Abmi7 | Db7 | Gb | Gb |
| Abmi7    A7 | D    Cmi7 F7 | Bb    Db7 | Gb |
| Abmi7    Emi7 A7 | D    Cmi7 F7 | Bb    Abmi7 Db7 | Gb |
| Abmi7 Db7    Emi7 A7 | D Bmi7    Cmi7 F7 | Bb Gmi7    Abmi7 Db7 | Gb |
| Bmi7 | E7 | A | A |
| Bmi7    C7 | F    Ab7 | Db    E7 | A |
| Bmi7    Gmi7 C7 | F    Ebmi7 Ab7 | Db    Bmi7 E7 | A |
| Bmi7 E7    Gmi7 C7 | F Dmi7    Ebmi7 Ab7 | Db Bbmi7    Bmi7 E7 | A |

Various chords can be altered in the chart, as in the following example:

Any chord in any column can be substituted for any other chord in the same vertical column, as in the following example:

For maximum variety memorize this chart with its combinatorial possibilities (which are astronomical!), such as in the following example:

$Dmi_7$ = D∅ or F or Bb (see substitutions for the minor 7th chord)

$G_7$ = $G_7^{(\#5)}$ or $G_7{}_{b5}^{b9}$ or $G_7{}_{\#5}^{\#9}$ or $G_7{}_{\#5}^{b9}$

C = Ami or A∅ or Gb

**SUGGESTED READING . . .**

*The Lydian Chromatic Concept of Tonal Organization* (pages 44-50) by George Russell
*The Professional Arranger Composer* by Russell Garcia
*Jazz: An Introduction to its Musical Basis* (chapter I) by Avril Dankworth
*Techniques of Twentieth Century Composition* (chapter 11) by Leon Dallin

**SUGGESTED LISTENING . . .**

*Giant Steps* by John Coltrane (Atlantic 1311). "Giant Steps" and "Countdown"
*Coltrane Jazz* by John Coltrane (Atlantic 1354). "Fifth House"
*Seven Steps to Heaven* by Miles Davis (Columbia CS 8851). "Basin Street Blues"

**SUGGESTED ASSIGNMENTS . . .**

1. Know the reasons for using chord substitutions.
2. Know the principle of chord substitution.
3. Write substitutions for any ten standards.
4. Explain and exemplify contextual substitution.

# Chapter XVI

# THE RHYTHM SECTION — PIANO

The rhythm section in jazz refers to the instruments in a jazz group which are normally entrusted with the time continuum. The rhythm section can include piano, organ, bass, guitar, drums, vibes, and/or miscellaneous percussion. For our purposes we will limit the rhythm section to piano, bass, and drums.

## THE PIANO

This chapter will concern itself primarily with two-hand voicings, voicings for the left hand, and other basic materials of jazz piano playing.

The role of the piano in the rhythm section is to provide harmonic ostinato; rhythmic impetus; contrapuntal interplay with the soloist; to provide introductions, interludes, and endings; and to be a soloist as well.

When the instrument is used as a solo instrument (primarily the right hand) utilize this book in the same manner as the other solo instruments.

### Some basic two-hand voicings

The main advantage to the minor seventh two-hand voicing in the following examples is that it affords six possibilities with minimum effort and movement; there are three possibilities with the II to $V_7$ root movement and three more possibilities with the II to bII root movement.

REGULAR RESOLUTION

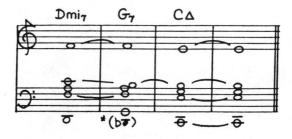

PARALLEL RESOLUTION

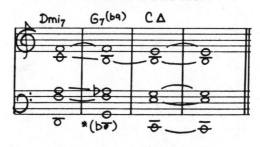

DIVERGENT RESOLUTION

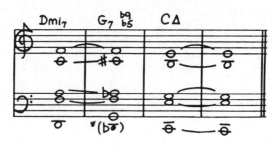

*The note in parentheses in these three examples, and all the other examples in this chapter, indicates an additional bass note option.

## II V₇ resolutions and inversions

The next sixteen examples present thirty-two more possibilities of simple, easily learned progressions.

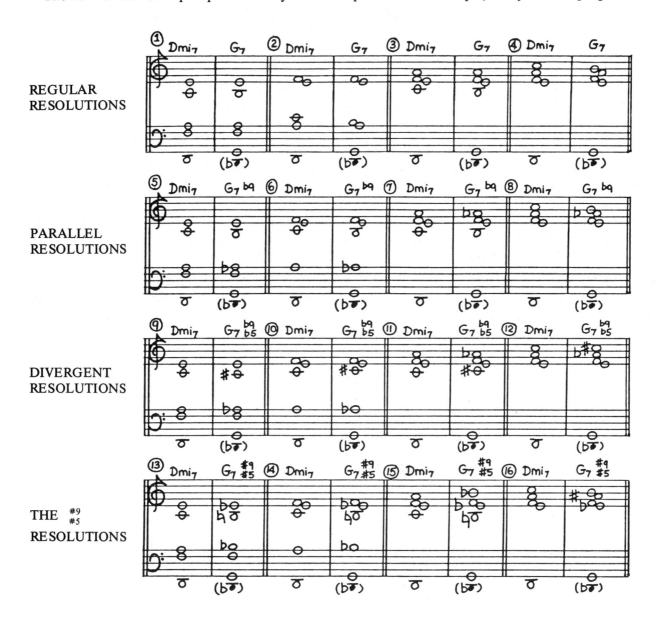

REGULAR
RESOLUTIONS

PARALLEL
RESOLUTIONS

DIVERGENT
RESOLUTIONS

THE #9
#5
RESOLUTIONS

## Extensions

Examples 1 through 4 present myriad other possibilities for voicing the basic II V₇ progression. Examples 1a, 1b, 2a, 2b, 3a, 3b, 4a, and 4b are models for further exploration which show various cluster possibilities using all of the other types of resolutions (regular, parallel, divergent, etc.).

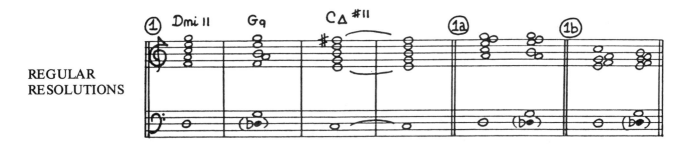

REGULAR
RESOLUTIONS

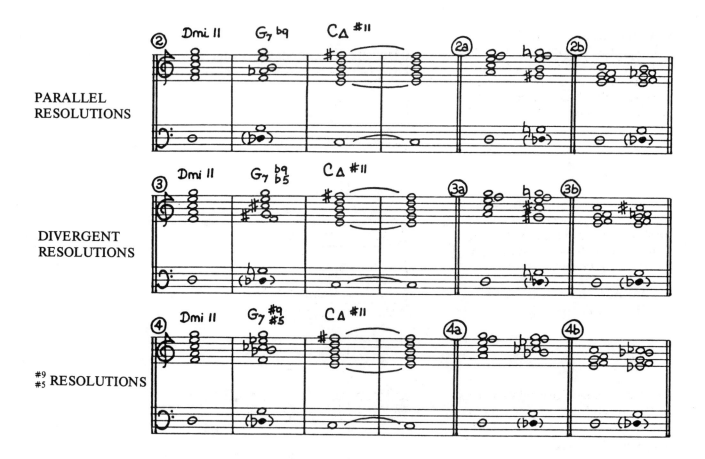

## Half diminished chords

To adapt the previous exercises for the half diminished chord simply lower the fifth in the minor seventh (II) chord.

## Rootless voicings

The rootless voicings offer more sophisticated possibilities for the II V₇ progression. In the left hand use the voicings and inversions which were in the right hand in the previous exercises (**Basic two-hand voicings, II V₇ resolutions and inversions**, etc.).

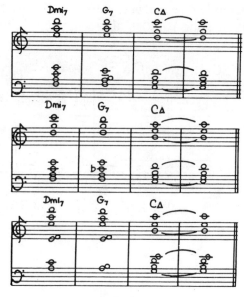

There are a few simple rules to be observed. In the minor seventh chord (II) avoid the major sixth above the root in the right hand voicing, as in the following example:

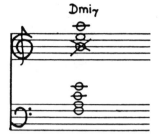

In the dominant seventh (V₇) avoid the perfect fourth above the root of the chord in the right hand voicing, as in the following example:

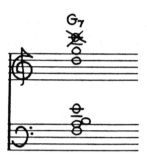

In the major chord (I) avoid the tonic and the perfect fourth above the root in the right hand voicing, as in the following examples:

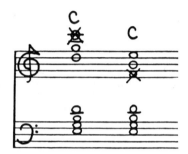

In place of the perfect fourth use the raised fourth, as in the following example:

## 'Comping chords for your own solos

All of the right hand voicings from the II V₇ resolutions and inversions should now be placed in the left hand and used for 'comping, as in the following examples:

## Shell voicings

These simple two-voice chords provide an easy way to realize changes in the left hand. Minor chords (II) are voiced 1-b7, dominant seventh chords (V₇) 1-b7 or 1-3, and major chords (I) 1-3 or 1-7 (or, more effectively, 1-5-7, using three voices). The following are some examples of shell voicings:

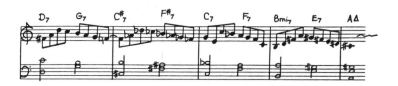

## Some simple blues voicings

Perhaps the simplest realization of the blues is a root in the left hand and the essential notes (3 and b7) in the right hand. With this voicing all movement in the right hand is by half step or whole step, as shown in the following example:

Next add a third voice to the chords, as in the following example:

Next try a simple "Charleston" rhythm and add a traditional turnaround, as in the following example:

For variety move up a half step on the offbeat, as in the following example:

For variety keep the same voicing (b7-3-6) for all chords, as in the following example:

Next try chromatic connecting chords, as in the following example:

For a fuller and more sophisticated two-hand voicing take the chords which were formerly in the right hand and transfer them to the left hand; then voice from the tonic of the chord down in perfect fourths in the right hand, keeping common tones like example #2, as shown in the following example:

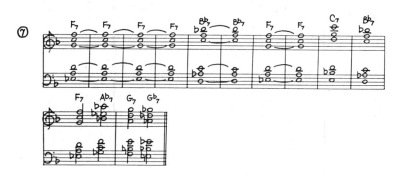

Next try using a constant voicing like example #5, as shown in the following example:

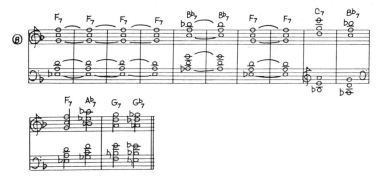

For basic blues, generally speaking, use the left hand voicings shown in example #9 for the keys of G, Gb, F, E, and Eb; use the voicings in example #10 for the keys of D, Db, C, B, Bb, A, and Ab.

95

To accompany your own solo lines use
voicings similar to those in examples
#7 and #8.


    All of the piano voicings should be played in all keys, all rhythms, all tempos, all meters and at all dynamic levels, using the appropriate and idiomatic dramatic devices.

    The pianist should listen to as many pianists as possible in an effort to find an idiomatic way to play his instrument both as an accompanist and as a soloist.

## SUGGESTED READING . . .

*Tonal and Rhythmic Principles* by John Mehegan

*Jazz Rhythm and the Improvised Line* by John Mehegan

*Swing and Early Progressive Styles* by John Mehegan

*Contemporary Piano Styles* by John Mehegan

*The Contemporary Jazz Pianist*, volumes 1 and 2 by Bill Dobbins

*Piano Voicings* by Jamey Aebersold

*Jazz Improvisation for Keyboard Players* by Dan Haerle

*Jazz/Rock Voicings for the Contemporary Keyboard Player* by Dan Haerle

*Topics in Jazz Piano Improvisation* by Lee Burswold

*Functional Piano for the Improviser* by John LaPorta

*Contemporary Keyboard Exercises* by David Chesky

## SUGGESTED LISTENING . . .

Recordings by Bud Powell, John Lewis, Horace Silver, Thelonious Monk, Oscar Peterson, Red Garland, Wynton Kelly, Tommy Flanagan, Barry Harris, Bill Evans, Billy Taylor, Herbie Hancock, McCoy Tyner, Cecil Taylor, et al.

## SUGGESTED ASSIGNMENTS . . .

1. Be able to play representative voicings from any of the examples.
2. Be able to handle these voicings in a variety of tunes.
3. Be able to handle the material from the rest of this book in conjunction with the voicings in this chapter.

# Chapter XVII

# THE BASS VIOL

In most pre-avant garde groups the prime function of the bass player has been to provide a harmonic and rhythmic ostinato in conjunction with the piano. The bass player has been traditionally assigned the task of "walking a line" built on the chords of the tune.

The basic rules for line building can be articulated and the following observations are the result of extended and prolonged observation of what is common practice with most of the best bass players.

The bass player should first do all the things in the previous chapters, particularly the exercises in the section that deals with learning to play cycles. He should practice cycles using repeated notes, perhaps two notes on each cycle member.

It seems in the normal run of compositions that there are probably three basic situations that the bass player may expect to encounter.

1. Changes that last one beat apiece. When the changes last a beat apiece, the most practical manner of realizing the line is to play the root of the chord on every beat.

2. If the changes last two beats apiece, then we have more possibilities. Standard practice has been to play the name of the chord on the beat.

3. Now, what to do with the interim beats or intermediate beats? One thing we might do is to approach each of the roots from a half step above. In other words we get from C to F by using a G$^b$ on the second beat of the measure.

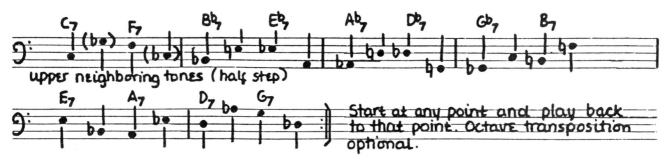

Another common practice is to come from a half step below. In other words, in going from C to F we use E on the second beat of the measure.

Another approach is from a whole step above the root tones; that is, in going from C to F, use G on the second beat of the measure.

Another technique with the two beat chords would be to play the fifth of the chord on the weak beats.

Another thing we might do is to put the note an octave above the root tones on the weak beats.

Although it is a bit more difficult, we might put the tenth (major or minor) on the weak beats of the measure.

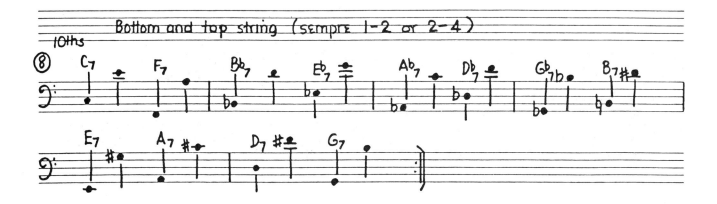

When we play changes built on something other than the circle of fourths these techniques become much more interesting because we lose some of the symmetry.

Of course, the bass player can mix the techniques. He can come from a half step above on one chord, a half step below on the next, then use a tenth and then an octave, etc.

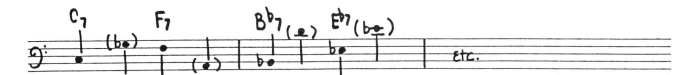

These are the essential ways of handling the two-beat chords.

What happens when the chord lasts a whole measure? The task set for us is now a bit more difficult because we have three beats to account for where nothing is written.

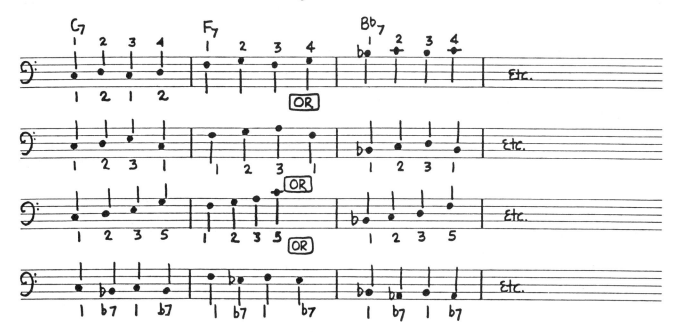

99

We might use roots and fifths.

OR

We might use triads, altering the third when necessary.

In all of the exercises in this chapter be sure to consider the quality of the chord:
Major versus minor
Augmented versus diminished
We might also use the entire chord.

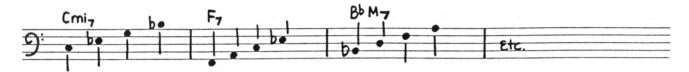

Now this brings us to the next point — the fact that we can walk the chords in various inversions or in a different order than usual.

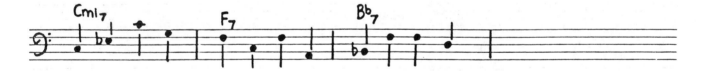

Another technique is to make sure we have the name of the chord on the beat and to use any notes we choose to get to the next chord.

We might use this approach: on beat one, the root of the chord; and on beat four, a leading tone to the next chord.

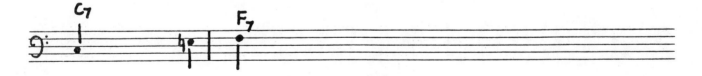

This leading tone could have been any one of the three mentioned before (upper or lower one half step or whole step above).

We must now consider what to do with beats two and three of the measure. It would be nice if we could walk right up the scale but that's impossible because we have too few notes to cover that much time. We would arrive at the note E on the third beat of the measure. This means, then, that we must either introduce a half step or an escape tone somewhere.

Practice joining the II V patterns to the turnbacks.

If the chord lasts more than a measure a different approach is necessary. This approach is often scalar. For instance, if the chord is a C major chord and it lasts for two measures there is no reason for the bass player to play C at the beginning of both measures. He might determine that his basic color is a C major scale and play C on the first beat of measure one and any colors from the C scale for the remaining seven beats.

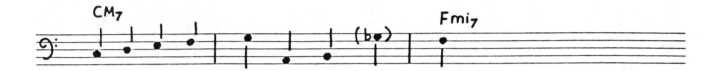

The leading tones should still be introduced on the beat before the chord changes.

It is also possible and desirable in this circumstance to use other scales to make the line. For instance, the bass player might choose the diminished scale for a II V$_7$ situation.

He might also choose the whole tone scale.

Another approach by modern bass players is to walk freely, usually in a chromatic manner, setting up the points of change of tonality only.

## A FEW HINTS ON PLAYING THE BLUES

Blues changes present special problems for bass players for a number of reasons. First, the extended measures of dominant seventh chords demand special attention. Some sort of scalar approach is demanded. Next, what is the bass player to do as far as turnbacks? Where might he introduce some II $V_7$ progressions to relieve the dominant seventh sound? How does the bass player avoid the trap of playing the same bass line over and over?

I will attempt to answer these and other questions that seem to plague young bass players when they play the blues. In approaching the blues the bass player should prepare a number of II $V_7$ formulae. The first one may occur in measure three and the next one in measures nine and ten. When this has been done then the II $V_7$ pattern may be realized in any one of the usual ways.

Next we may use a turnback of some sort in measures eleven and twelve.

Next we should set up leading tones to each change of chord.

103

Now we need to fill in the missing notes. We might fill the chords in this way: use the major scale to which the dominant seventh chord in question belongs as a basis, i.e., $F_7$ = the Bb major scale, $Bb_7$ = the Eb major scale, and so on.

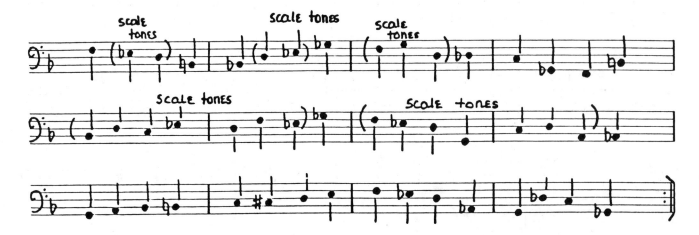

Here is another version set up the same way.

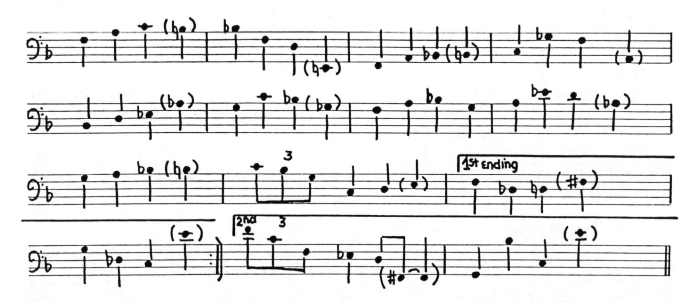

The player is urged to experiment and to use the blues substitution chart to obtain other change possibilities on which to build lines.

Another approach to the blues which allows the player to keep the basic changes involves a kind of chord running.

Yet another approach allows a bass player to remain in a single position for the entire blues. This technique as a special circumstance allows the player to play the blues in any key using the same fingering and hand position. For example, by moving the whole hand to another position we can immediately play the blues in another key. Practice the following example in all keys. Stay in one position; use no open strings.

Another possibility involves the use of a single type of scale color for each dominant seventh chord. For instance, the bass player may decide to use the diminished scale to realize each dominant seventh in the blues.

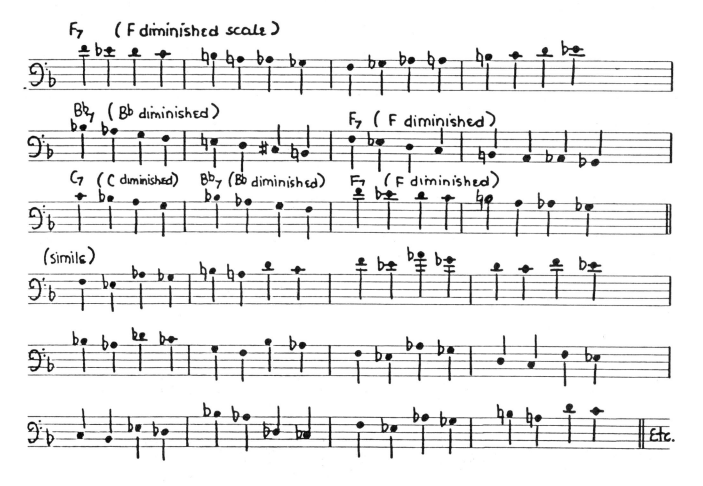

The main object in all of these exercises is to play a musical line with direction, forward motion and purpose.

The bass player should study the work of other bass players for "drop offs," rhythm accents and other idiomatic devices.

Four other major concepts that the modern bass player should be aware of are:

1. Fret or position playing.
2. Left hand pizzicati.
3. Multiple fingered plucking.
4. Slides.

In concept number one, the bass player takes advantage of the fact that all of the strings are the same interval apart, a perfect fourth. This means that like structures can be played in like manner. For instance, it is possible to play any major scale with the same fingering provided the open strings are avoided.

This also happens with chords, intervals, etc.

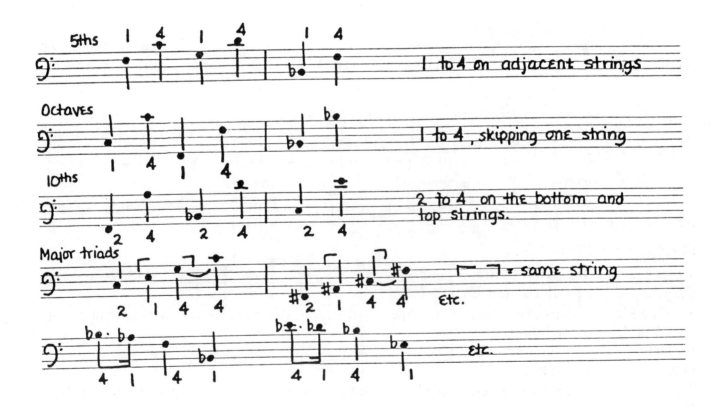

Caution: watch intonation as the size of the intervals gets smaller in the upper positions.

In concept number two, the left hand is used to pluck the strings. This is done for a number of reasons, such as increased facility, change of basic tone color, etc. If the note to be sounded is an open string, just pluck with any finger.

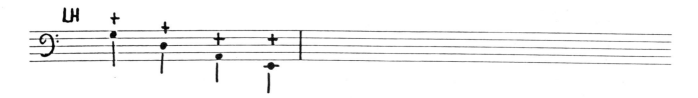

If the note is a stopped note this technique works better if the stopped note is with the first finger. We can then pluck a half step second finger to first finger or a whole step fourth finger to first finger.

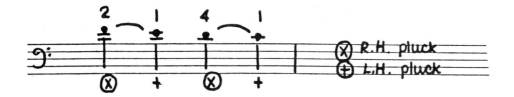

The third concept involves the alternation of the fingers of the right hand in walking and solo playing.

The fourth concept, sliding, is possible only when all of the notes involved are on the same string. The first of a series of notes is attacked (plucked), and because the string is still vibrating we can slide to other notes.

In actual performance all four of these concepts are usually combined to make music. The bass player should also spend a considerable amount of time with the Chapter VIII, Turnbacks.

**SUGGESTED READING . . .**

*A Jazz Improvisation Method for Stringed Instruments. Volume Two: Cello and Bass Viol* by David Baker

*Comprehensive Bass Method* by Ron Carter

*Ron Carter Bass Lines* transcribed from volume 6 (*All Bird*) of Jamey Aebersold's series of play-along records *A New Approach to Jazz Improvisation*

*Improvising Jazz Bass* by Rick Laird

*Bebop Bass* by Harold Miller

*The Monk Montgomery Electric Bass Method* by Monk Montgomery. Edited and compiled by David Baker.

*The Evolving Bassist* by Rufus Reid

*Evolving Upward* by Rufus Reid

*Rufus Reid Bass Lines* transcribed from volume 1 (*A New Approach to Jazz Improvisation*) and volume 2 (*Nothin' But Blues*) of Jamey Aebersold's series of play-along records *A New Approach to Jazz Improvisation*

## SUGGESTED LISTENING . . .

*Walkin'* by Miles Davis (Prestige LP 7076).  Percy Heath.

*Milestones* by Miles Davis (Columbia CS 9428).  Paul Chambers.

*Kind of Blue* by Miles Davis (Columbia CS 8163).  Paul Chambers.

*The Shape of Jazz to Come* by Ornette Coleman (Atlantic AT 1317).  Charlie Haden.

*Miles Smiles* by Miles Davis (Columbia CS 9401).  Ron Carter.

*Heavy Sounds* by Elvin Jones (Impulse A-9161).  Richard Davis.

## SUGGESTED ASSIGNMENTS . . .

1.  Learn at least two new tunes a day.
2.  Practice walking the cycle in as many ways as possible.
3.  Work for sound and ease of production.
4.  Practice soloing like a horn player.  Avoid walking and playing quarter notes in your solo line.

# Chapter XVIII

# DRUMS

The drummer functions in different ways in different groups.  Some of the things that determine how he is to function are: style of group, size of group, abilities of the group, era which it represents, and many other musical and non-musical factors.

Traditionally there seem to be certain functions assigned to a drummer and these functions vary only in degree.  The first function is to provide a rhythmic time continuum.  This is usually done by assigning certain uses to certain parts of the set.  The four main parts are:

1.  Hi-hat cymbal         3.  Bass drum
2.  Ride cymbal          4.  Snare drum

The hi-hat (sock) cymbal usually plays on beats two and four in 4/4 time, on beats two and three or on beat two in 3/4 time. etc.

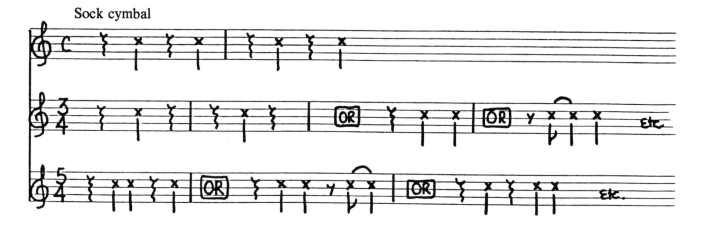

The ride or top cymbal is usually assigned the main figure implying the basic time.

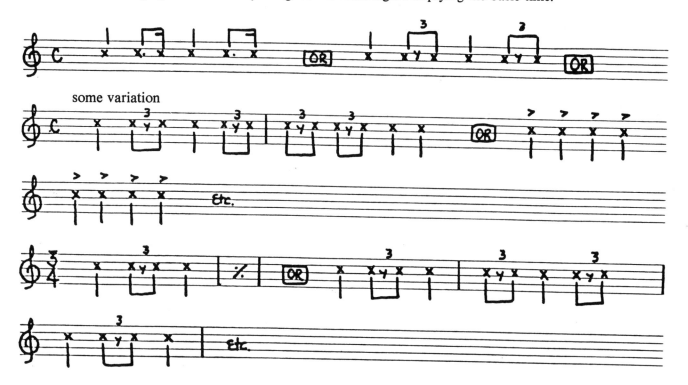

The bass drum plays either four beats or two beats to the bar in 4/4 time and is usually used for punctuation and emphasis.

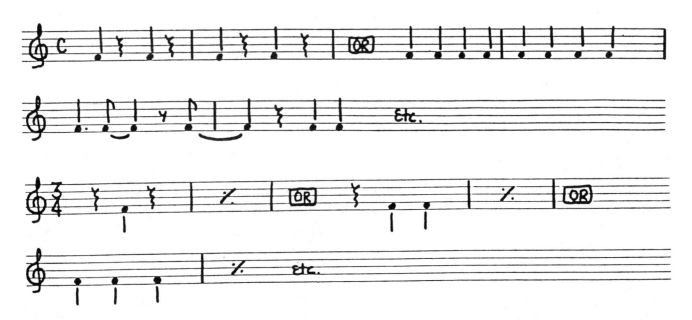

The left hand on the snare drum is usually assigned the task of playing fills, accenting with the soloist or a section, or in general, serving as a free agent.

Here is a short example of what the typical drum part would look like with hi-hat, ride cymbal, bass drum, and snare drum going simultaneously:

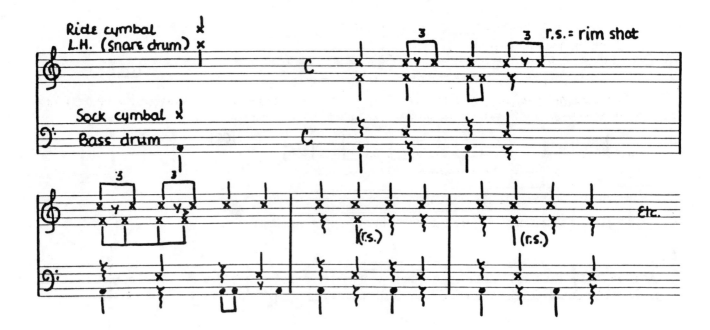

Another function that the good drummer performs is to help outline the form of the tune. He accomplishes this in a number of ways, some of which are:

1. The use of rolls and/or accents to indicate the endings and beginnings of sections of tunes.

2. Change of color (using different combinations of instruments, different dynamic levels, different rhythmic configurations, etc.) for different sections of the tune.

3. Relating to the basic time continuum in a different way in each section of the tune.

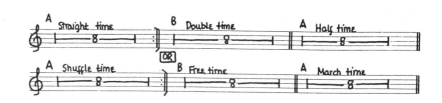

The good drummer will also explore the different ways in which he can relate to the soloist. This, of course, presupposes that he is a listening drummer.

1. He might play with the soloist, catching his rhythmic figures, observing his dynamics, matching his intensity, density and generally anticipating his direction.

Examples: Soloist — Busy, complex, intense, ff
Drummer — Busy, complex, intense, ff
(or matching less than all four factors)

2. He might counter the soloist.

Examples: Soloist — Busy, complex, intense, ff, double time
Drummer — relaxed, simple, low level intensity, pp, half time

3. His relationship might vary from section to section. The drummer might also explore a different form grouping (example A) or different metric grouping (example B) than the soloist.

Example A: Soloist ⊢— 6 —⊣⊢— 6 —⊣
Drummer ⊢—— 12 ——⊣

Example B: Soloist: 48 beats grouped in $\frac{4}{4}$ ⟶ 12 measures of 4
Drummer: 48 beats grouped in $\frac{6}{4}$ ⟶ 8 measures of 6

Above all, the drummer must play in a manner consistent with the style, era, and thrust of the group. All things should be done with the thought of making music as the highest goal.

## SUGGESTED READING . . .

*A Manual for the Modern Drummer* by Don De Michael and Alan Dawson
*The Art of Modern Jazz Drumming* by Jack De Johnette and Charlie Perry
*Brush Artistry* by Philly Joe Jones
*Brush Fire* by Willis Kirk

## SUGGESTED LISTENING . . .

*Workin' and Steamin'* by Miles Davis (Prestige P-24034)
*Milestones* by Miles Davis (Columbia CL 1193)
*Freedom Jazz Dance* by Miles Davis (Columbia CL 2601)
*Nefertiti* by Miles Davis (Columbia CS 9594)
*Kind of Blue* by Miles Davis (Columbia PC 8163)

## SUGGESTED ASSIGNMENTS . . .

1. Study, analyze, and play with your favorite drummers via recordings.
2. Practice basic patterns in all meters and at all tempi, dynamic, and intensity levels.
3. Study!!!

# Chapter XIX

# A PSYCHOLOGICAL APPROACH TO COMMUNICATING THROUGH AN IMPROVISED SOLO

One of the most neglected areas in jazz has to do with the use of psychological principles, such as the use of certain musical devices to elicit specific emotional responses. Such concepts are utilized on a different level in movie and television background writing.

In the course of history, certain musical qualities have become symbols of human acts and feelings. Carroll C. Pratt in his book *The Meaning of Music* says: "Human action is a pattern of motion with velocity, direction, strength, and tempo. Smooth, powerful, regular motion is a sign of successful functioning. Whenever the human organism does function well, whether it be in mind or body, there arises feeling of pleasure. Now the beholder of such motion through association with his own experience also finds it pleasant, and should he concentrate on the appearance of the motion itself, that is, see it or hear it aesthetically, he will call it graceful or beautiful.

"Violent, spasmodic fluctuating action, on the other hand, signifies imperfect functions, imperfect control of action, and it is accompanied by feelings of unpleasantness, anger, fear, frustration, and anxiety. There is some ground for suspecting a correspondence between the motion of human action and the emotion in our apprehension of such action."

Harry S. Broudy, in *A Realistic Philosophy of Music Education,* pursues the idea further: "If musical motion is analogous to the movement of human action, it can express the emotion accompanying the action. In other words, we associate specific emotion with certain tonal movements — if the listener knows the nature of the action or feeling portrayed and the artist has captured the characteristic motion of the action in tonal motion, and if no subjective psychological factors intervene, then a careful, cultivated listening may result in the awareness of this specific significance."

It is my belief that the prime purpose of all music is to communicate, i.e., to project certain feelings, attitudes, etc., to a listener. Carroll Pratt says it this way: "The expression of emotional life may not be the final object of music, if to be final means to be decisive or single to the exclusion of all other possibilities, but it is beyond doubt one very important and frequent aspect of tonal forms."

What do the preceding paragraphs mean to the jazz musician? What kind of directions do they indicate? They might suggest that a certain type of musical solo or line will affect most listeners in a certain way.

For example, a diatonic line with strongly enunciated rhythms and symmetrical shape will probably elicit a response of pleasure or fulfillment; or conversely, an asymmetrical line full of angularity, sudden accents and unpredictable volume changes will elicit a response of anxiety, uneasiness, etc. The good jazz player must learn to manipulate the emotions of the listener.

To indicate further how the jazz player might go about eliciting certain feelings using musical materials void of programatic intention, I again quote Carroll C. Pratt: "A recent very excellent experimental study of the effects of music shows, at one point, the difficulties created by not considering the possibility that the emotions "accompanying the music" or "suggested by" the music were in all strictness qualities inherent in the music itself.

"The listeners were told to make note of any emotions or words suggested by the composition. These emotional states were referred to as playful, whimsical, triumphant, powerful, martial, majestic, calm, peaceful, hurrying, restless, struggling, bewildering, tumultuous, uncertain, suspenseful, etc. Most of those words, when used for subjective moods, stand for psychological experiences which include among their components various forms of movement. In so far as similar movements may be presented tonally, the same words apply equally well to musical effects. A person says, for example, that he feels restless. A description of what it feels like to be restless might include references to such things as increased rate of breathing and heartbeat, unsteady organics in the region of the diaphragm, tapping of the feet or fingers, inability to keep still, etc. It requires no great knowledge of music to appreciate the fact that much the same kind of movement may easily be produced in musical phrases. Staccato, crescendos, shakes, wide jumps in pitch — all such devices conduce to the creation of an auditing structure which is appropriately described as restless."

The preceding represents only one of a multiplicity of viewpoints concerned with the way music affects us. Many of the viewpoints have overlap and **all** hold something of value for the jazz musician.

Another viewpoint deals with responses that are, by and large, conditioned or the product of the acculturation process. This viewpoint presupposes a common fund of knowledge and certain musical norms common to the player and the listener. Most people in a western culture respond in a similar manner to a rousing march or at least they are not likely to feel an inclination to waltz or jitterbug. Because of conditioning we also perceive Chopin's Funeral March as sad, tragic, somber, melancholy or some similar feeling rather than happy, gay, ebullient, etc.

A concept that might be classified under the first viewpoint is one that relates tension to extremes in volume, density, speed and complexity. The view held is that any pronounced change to the plus side of any one or all of the above factors will produce tension. This tension might be read by the listener as anxiety, anger, etc.

If we view this same concept as belonging to viewpoint two we would perceive these factors not as fast, loud, etc., by abstraction but rather according to a norm (i.e., not fast but faster than – – –, not loud but louder than – – –). In other words, if a jazz player, in the midst of a relatively placid situation, doubles the time or introduces an extended passage of notes faster than the basic unit of the time the listener perceives this as a feeling of tension (anxiety, anger, etc.).

Another notion that the jazz player must examine is the concept of tension produced by high notes. It seems that this concept may be somewhat reconciled to the first viewpoint. Although there is nothing inherent in a change of frequency to suggest tension, experience seems to bear out the fact that tension is elicited. This phenomenon may have evolved because of the physical strain and expenditure of energy which results in the production of high notes for a vocalist and our tendency to empathize.

Consistent with the second viewpoint would be the concept of tension produced through the use of consonance and dissonance. (This concept presupposes some broad area of agreement about what is consonant and what is dissonant.) Within our culture the consensus is that movement from consonance to dissonance or of dissonance to greater dissonance creates tension. The converse is also true. This knowledge enables the jazzman to work with consonance and dissonance in such a way so as to elicit feelings related to tension (anxiety, anger, etc.) or feelings related to lack of tension (contentment, euphoria, etc.).

A rising line tends to create tension and the longer it rises the more tension it creates. The main reason is that the longer a line continues in the same direction, the more we anticipate a change. If the change of direction occurs, our expectations are fulfilled and we experience a release from the tension (pleasure, happiness, etc.). If our expectations are not fulfilled our desires are thwarted and we are frustrated, disappointed and ultimately bored.

In line with viewpoint two is the concept of using resolution expectancy or resolution tendency to produce tension. In this concept, conditioning leads us to expect certain notes in particular scale systems to react in specific ways; for instance, the tendency of the leading tone (seventh degree) to resolve up or the dominant seventh (fourth degree) to resolve down a step in the major - minor system. When the resolution takes place we experience pleasure, when it does not we experience frustration.

There is another concept consistent with viewpoint two, very simply stated; when a wide area of pitch and dynamic range is covered in a brief span of time, tension results. (i.e., covering three octaves, going from ppp to fff in two measures, whole note = 180.) This tension results because of the analogy between energy and speed. (i.e., it takes more energy to go 100 yards in nine seconds than it does to go 100 yards in nine minutes.)

While there is some disagreement among musicians about the validity of some of these concepts, my own feeling is that music is the language of the emotions. It misses its main reason for being if it fails to arouse a genuine emotion and pleasurable expansion. Of course music (i.e., auditory perception) is no more emotion than the letters B-L-A-C-K are the visual sensation of that color. It is the language that arouses the subjective experience. What language could be more suitable than one whose forms are similar to the objects to be expressed?

There are many other such concepts that are of import to the jazz musician. The primary purpose of this chapter has been to open up some new areas for the jazz player.

## SUGGESTED READING . . .

*The Meaning of Music* by Carroll C. Pratt

*The Basis of Criticism in the Arts* (Formistic Criticism) by Stephen C. Pepper

*A Realistic Philosophy of Music Education* by Harry S. Broudy. In the *National Society for the Study of Education Yearbook.*

*Santayana and the Sense of Beauty* by Willard E. Arnett

*Feeling and Form* by Susanne K. Langer

*Shaping Forces in Music* by Ernest Toch

*Aesthetic Quality* by Stephen C. Pepper

*A Composer's World* (Chapter II) by Paul Hindemith

## SUGGESTED LISTENING...

*Porgy and Bess* by Miles Davis and Gil Evans (Columbia CL 1274)

*Sketches of Spain* by Miles Davis and Gil Evans (Columbia CS 8271)

*Ornette Coleman at Town Hall* by Ornette Coleman (ESP 1006): "Sadness"

*Mingus/Oh Yeah* by Charles Mingus (Atlantic LP 1377): "Passions of a Man"

*Ascension* by John Coltrane (Impulse AS-95)

*Dogon A. D.* by Julius Hemphill (Mbari 5001)

*Unit Structures* by Cecil Taylor (Blue Note 84237)

*Airlore* by Air (Arista AN 3014)

*Les Stances à Sophie* by the Art Ensemble of Chicago (Pathé (F) C062-11365)

*Living Time* by George Russell (Columbia KC 31490)

*Steppin'* by the World Saxophone Quartet (Black Saint BSR 27)

## SUGGESTED ASSIGNMENTS . . .

1.  Restate in your own words the concepts advanced in this chapter.
2.  Find specific examples on recordings of these concepts.
3.  Read other books on the allied subjects.

# Chapter XX

# SOME ADVANCED CONCEPTS IN JAZZ PLAYING

In the last decade much has happened to jazz playing. Harmonic resources have expanded. Rhythmic concepts have broadened. There has been a growing awareness of drama in music and there have been growing inclinations to make use of the entire spectrum of musical colors and sounds.

Although many jazz players deny a place in jazz to such techniques as twelve tone playing, electronic music, strict forms of chance music and system music, it may be that increasing familiarity might render them adaptable and acceptable to jazz.

It is not within the scope of this chapter to discuss these diverse techniques. They are more well handled in many books (usually non-jazz) on composition and related topics. Rather, I intend to discuss some relatively new melodic, harmonic and rhythmic concepts that are being used with some success by modern players.

I.   The concepts that deal with melody are:
1. Intervallic playing
2. Directional playing
3. Pure melody or poly-modal playing
4. Color on color
5. Extreme angularity

II.   The concepts that are harmonic are:
1. Functional substitution
2. Chord tonic chromaticism

III.   The rhythmic concepts are:
1. Regrouping within the time
2. Free time against stable time
3. Free time
4. Accelerando against: accelerando, prevailing time, slow time
5. Prevailing time against: accelerando, prevailing time, slow down
6. Slow down against: accelerando, prevailing time, slow down
7. Double time, one third time and other divisions of the existing time (stable ratio)

## I. Melodic Concepts

1. Intervallic playing: In the concept of intervallic playing, the interval becomes the means as well as the end. In this concept, the player arbitrarily, or with some other consideration in mind, decides on a set of intervals and uses them consistently for the duration of a tune. I have found that I have more success when I either limit the number of intervals or stick with one type of interval to the exclusion of others. In the first instance a player might choose a half step and a perfect fourth. He will then combine them in any manner he chooses, irrespective of the underlying harmonic structure. He might use a series of half steps followed by a perfect fourth.

He might use a perfect fourth, two half steps, another perfect fourth, etc.

He might choose a random combination, which is usually the case.

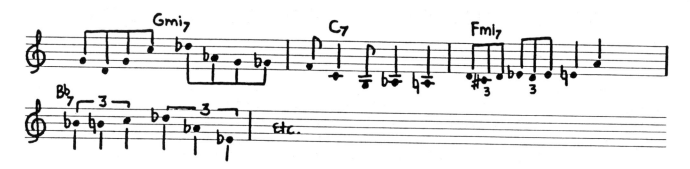

The intervals chosen might be a minor third and a tritone.

When playing in this manner the player may also use the inversions of an interval (i.e., minor third inverts to Major sixth). He may also use three or four intervals although this is more difficult (i.e., half step, minor third, perfect fourth and Major second). He may also link sets of intervals with a foreign interval. Use a Major third and a perfect fourth.

Even more practical for the jazz player is the notion of using this technique in a much freer fashion, i.e., a half step followed by a skip, or better yet, a stepwise move, half or whole, followed by a skip.

In this technique the ultimate would be to have a set of intervals predominate a section of the tune. The player would play either in a free or a structured manner but would concentrate on the one or two intervals which are predetermined.

In the second instance the player might choose one class of intervals (i.e., a perfect fourth) and build the whole chorus or section of a chorus around it. The inversions and alterations are also permissible i.e., fourth, fifth, tritone and sharp five.

Again, a more practical use of this technique would be to play a melody, either free or structured, but have a single interval (in this case a fourth) predominating.

Some recorded examples of this kind of tune would be:

"Freedom Jazz Dance" (The perfect fourth) E. Harris
"Blue Monk" (The third) T. Monk
"Misterioso" (The sixth) T. Monk
"Stratusphunk" (The sixth) G. Russell

In using this technique the player might ask: why one set of intervals as opposed to another? First, the player might decide to use the set of intervals that predominate the written composition that he is playing. This, of course, contributes to a sense of cohesion in the improvised chorus because of the similarity of material between the improvisation and the melody itself.

Another reason for choosing a set of intervals would be a preference on the part of a player for those particular intervals. I particularly like the combination of a skip plus a half step, because of the built-in tension and release factor inherent in this combination.

Another reason might be the desire to play in a flowing manner or an angular manner (i.e., diatonic movement suggests flow and skips suggest angularity).

For those who wonder why this approach doesn't sound wrong since we are not consciously observing the chords, hear this:

a. When the intervals are consistent, the listener tends to hear according to his own preferences. He perceives dissonant intervals as the most important intervals if he hears "outside". He hears consonant intervals as being the most important if he hears "inside".

b. In many ways playing a jazz chorus is like any other artistic endeavor; that is, essentially a case of problem solving. Once the use of a particular set of intervals has been established to the ear of the listener as the problem, then the success or failure of the jazz chorus becomes dependent on how successfully the intervals are used. In other words, the realization of vertical structures becomes a secondary consideration to the successful manipulation of the chosen intervals.

2. Directional playing: This refers to a technique which involves the use of two scales of the same quality alternately. (Both Major, both whole tone, etc.) Arbitrarily impose a scale on a chord; when the chord changes, go to the alternate scale. Continue alternating each time the chord changes. Although theoretically any scale quality will work, in practice the technique works best with the symmetrical scales (whole tone, diminished or chromatic scales). For the example the two whole tone scales are used.

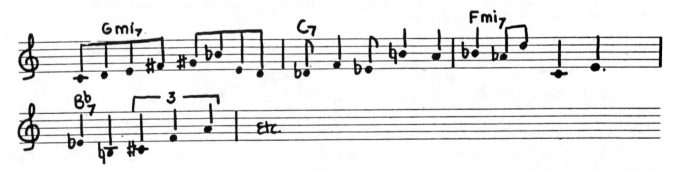

The assumption is that in many instances the listener is more aware of a quantitative than a qualitative change; he hears a change of scale rather than the type of scale to which it changes.

3. Pure melody or poly-modal playing: In this concept, melody takes precedence over all other considerations. The player concentrates on constructing endless melody or melodies that might embrace many keys and modes simultaneously. No obeisance is made to vertical or horizontal structures that conflict with the melody as it is conceived. In general this technique is most successful in the area of "free" (without changes) playing. Most of the best players in the avant garde embrace this concept or some modified form of it. Listen to Ornette Coleman, Archie Shepp, Charles Tyler, Albert Ayler and others.

4. Color relations: This concept stated simply, means using intersecting horizontal or vertical colors in a number of different ways. For instance, it is possible to color the degrees of a Major scale with other Major scales.

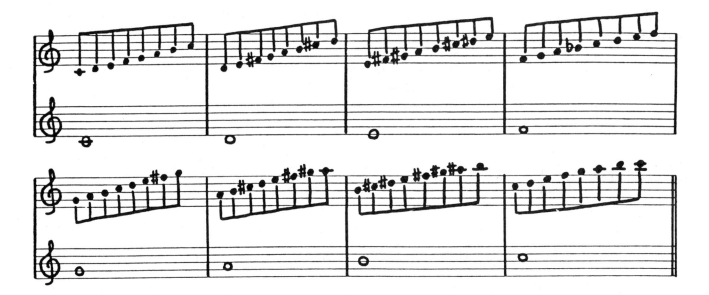

This technique could be employed in static situations. For example, when the player decides to color a Dmi$_7$, which lasts indefinitely, with a C Major scale he might set up a color on color situation by maintaining the Major scale of C as a cantus firmus and coloring it with the Major scales built on the diatonic degrees of the scale.

It is also possible to color the degrees of the Major scale with any other scale, triad or seventh color. The player could color Major scales with augmented triads

or diminished scales.

The number of combinations is astronomical:

| | | | |
|---|---|---|---|
| Whole tone | Major | Diminished | Ascending melodic minor |
| Major | Diminished | Diminished/whole tone | Blues |

5. Extreme angularity: This concept refers to the idea of using octave displacements to destroy a diatonic line by arbitrarily putting notes in different octaves.

A is the original line.
B is the line made disjunct.

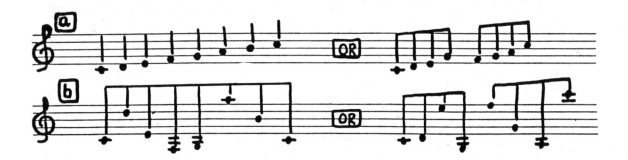

The most commonplace line will take on new interest with this technique. Obviously, this technique is more difficult for some instruments than others.

## II. Harmonic Concepts

1. Functional substitution: Functional substitution means substituting for any chord any other chord of the same quality. (i.e., for $Gmi_7$ substitute $Bbmi_7$, $Abmi_7$, $Dmi_7$, or $G_7$ for $Db_7$, $A_7$, $B_7$, etc.)

This concept relies very heavily on the notion that the ear is more apt to hear function than actual quality. That is, if the chord operates from within the proper place in the $II\ V_7\ I$ formula, the listener hears it as the proper chord.

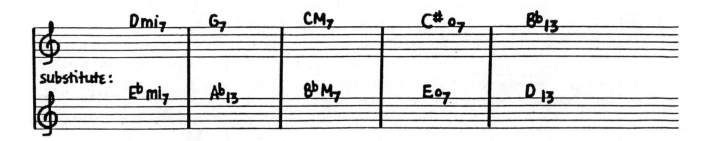

2. Chord tonic chromaticism: This refers to the practice of using chromatic scales starting on the tonic of the chord to color every chord in a composition.

The notes of the chromatic scale do not have to be consecutive and intervals larger than a half step may be introduced as long as the general and main impression is one of chromaticism that originates from the root of the chord.

## III. Rhythmic Concepts

1. Regrouping within the time: This concept is particularly useful when the vertical structures are clearly and strongly defined and the structure is relatively conventional.

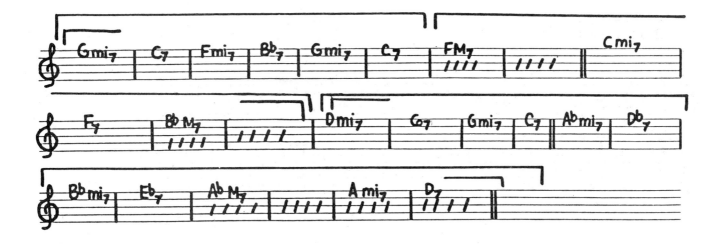

The grouping as it stands is <sup>A</sup>⊢— 8 —⊣ <sup>B</sup>⊢— 8 —⊣ <sup>C</sup>⊢— 8 —⊣ . The soloist as well as the rhythm section would do musical things to point up the beginning and ending of each of the eight-measure segments. The soloist would probably start his melodies and phrases either on the first or fifth measure of one of the eight-measure segments. He would probably signal the end of an eight-measure segment by tapering off or building into the next eight-measure segment. Whatever means employed he would probably, consciously or subconsciously because of tradition, do something to delineate the form of the composition.

If the player wanted to regroup the bars, there are many ways to regroup a twenty-four measure structure — two groups of twelve, four groups of six, six groups of four or any number of odd groupings, nine plus nine plus six, or seven plus seven plus ten. To effect such a regrouping, the player must then really think in the new grouping, i.e., starting melodies in measure thirteen and tapering at the end of twenty-four.

2. Free time: This can be done in any type of tune, vertical or otherwise. In this technique the player plays across the time but generally without being in a sub-division of the time. For instance, avoid playing in a time that is twice the time, one half the time, one third of time, etc.

What does the player do about the changes while all of this is taking place? One procedure would be to keep one ear glued to the prevailing time (the rhythm section) and make the changes as they occur in the rhythm section; in other words, playing more or less tonally.

SOLOIST

RHYTHM   $G_7$ ⊢— 8 —⊣  $Ab_7$ ⊢— 4 —⊣  $Db_7$ ⊢— 4 —⊣  $Bmi_7$ ⊢— 8 —⊣

Another procedure might involve using intervallic playing, pure melody or some other technique. Some of these techniques would relieve the player of the responsibility of having to consciously and specifically relate to the chords.

3. The other side of this coin would have both the soloist and the rhythm section playing freely with no pre-arranged tempo or meter. Prevailing circumstances would dictate the direction of the musical proceedings.

| | **Soloist** | **Rhythm** |
|---|---|---|
| a. | Accelerando | Accelerando<br>prevailing time<br>slow time |
| b. | Prevailing time | Accelerando<br>prevailing time<br>slow down |
| c. | Slow down | Accelerando<br>prevailing time<br>slow down |

Numbers four, five and six represent the ways in which the horn player can relate to the rhythm section. Numbers four and six are the two in which the soloist is actively involved in initiating the change of relationship.

| 4. | Soloist | Soloist speeds up |
| | Rhythm | Speeds up |
| | Soloist | Speeds up |
| | Rhythm | Stays constant |
| | Soloist | Speeds up |
| | Rhythm | Slows down |
| 5. | Soloist | Stays constant |
| | Rhythm | Speeds up |
| | | Stays constant |
| | | Slows down |
| 6. | Soloist | Slows down |
| | Rhythm | Speeds up |
| | | Stays constant |
| | | Slows down |

In each case the soloist may move toward an undetermined speed or he may move from the constant time through several choruses until he arrives at a double time, or he may start at the double time and move toward the constant time or on past to the slow time which might be the prevailing time. The player will, of course, examine other possibilities.

The effect can be very exciting as the soloist begins to move away from the prevailing time. The first impression is that the soloist is rushing the time until the listener becomes aware of the purpose of the accelerando. As the soloist approaches double time the excitement continues to build until the time is again in juxtaposition. The same theory takes place on the trip back to the original time.

7. Both double time and other divisions of the existing time: Double time, which refers to the practice of using the sixteenth note as the basic unit instead of the eighth note and half time, which is the practice of using the quarter note as the basic unit, are in common use by most jazzmen of today. The technique of playing with the dotted quarter, or the dotted half as the basic unit, are relatively unexplored areas.

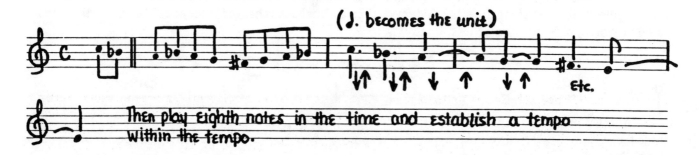

Likewise in the following two examples:

(a) In the second measure each of the six notes in the triplets becomes a unit of the new time. Then this is broken into eighth notes or even smaller units.

(b) Each of the triplets becomes one measure of $\frac{3}{4}$ in the new time.

## SUGGESTED READING . . .

*The Lydian Chromatic Concept of Tonal Organization for Improvisation* by George Russell
*Free Jazz* by Ekkehard Jost
*Black Nationalism and the Revolution in Music* by Frank Kofsky
*Jazz in the Sixties* by Michael Budds

## SUGGESTED LISTENING . . .

*Love Cry* by Albert Ayler (Impulse AS-9165)
*Time Changes* by David Brubeck (Columbia CS-2127)
*The Empty Foxhole* by Ornette Coleman (Blue Note BLP 4246)
*Ascension* by John Coltrane (Impulse AS-95)
*How Time Passes* by Don Ellis (Candid LP 8004)
*Dogon A.D.* by Julius Hemphill (Mbari 5001)
*Abstractions* by Gunther Schuller (Atlantic SD 1365)
*Air* by Cecil Taylor (Barnaby 230562)
*Unit Structures* by Cecil Taylor (Blue Note 84237)
*Airlore* by Air (Arista AN 3014)
*Urban Bushman* by the Art Ensemble of Chicago (ECM 2-1211)
*Crystal Texts* by James Newton and Anthony Davis (Moers Music 01048)
*Living Time* by George Russell (Columbia KC 31490)
*Folk and Mystery Stories* by Charles Tyler (Sonet SNTF-849)
*Dedication* by David Liebman (CMP 9 ST)

## SUGGESTED ASSIGNMENTS . . .

1. Be able to define and exemplify the concepts put forth in this chapter.
2. Be able to list players and records that contain examples of some of these concepts.
3. Choose a few standards and regroup them in various ways.
4. List players of your instrument in avant garde style and group them according to which of the above concepts they use.

---

# BIBLIOGRAPHY

Aebersold, Jamey. The Jamey Aebersold Play-Along Series: *A New Approach to Jazz Improvisation.* Series volumes listed as follows: volume 1: *A New Approach to Jazz Improvisation*; volume 2: *Nothin' But Blues*; volume 3: *The II/V7/I Progression*; volume 4: *Movin' On*; volume 5: *Time to Play Music*; volume 6: *All Bird*; volume 7: *Miles Davis*; volume 8: *Sonny Rollins*; volume 9: *Woody Shaw*; volume 10: *David Baker*; volume 11: *Herbie Hancock*; volume 12: *Duke Ellington*; volume 13: *Cannonball Adderley*; volume 14: *Benny Golson*; volume 15: *Payin' Dues*; volume 16: *Turnarounds, Cycles, and II/V7/Is*; volume 17: *Horace Silver*; volume 18: *Horace Silver* (Intermediate/Advanced); volume 19: *David Liebman*; volume 20: *Jimmy Raney*; volume 21: *Gettin' It Together*; volume 22: *13 Favorite Standards*; volume 23: *One Dozen Standards*; volume 24: *Major & Minor*; volume 25: *17 All-Time Standards*; volume 26: *The Scale Syllabus*; volume 27: *John Coltrane*; volume 28: *John Coltrane.* New Albany, Indiana: Jamey Aebersold.

_____. *Transcribed Piano Voicings: (Comping) to the Record "A New Approach to Jazz Improvisation, volume 1," As Played By Jamey Aebersold on the Volume 1 Record.* New Albany, Indiana: Jamey Aebersold, 1980.

Aebersold, Jamey and Slone, Ken, transcribers and editors. *Charlie Parker Omnibook.* Atlantic Music Corp., 1978. Collection of transcriptions of Charlie Parker solos.

Arnett, Willard E. *Santayana and the Sense of Beauty.* Indiana University Press, 1955-57.

Baker, David N. *Advanced Ear Training for the Jazz Musician.* Lebanon, Indiana: Studio P/R, Inc., 1977.

_____. *Advanced Improvisation.* 3 volumes. Bloomington, Indiana: Frangipani Press, 1974.

_____. *Contemporary Techniques for the Trombone.* 2 volumes. New York: Charles Colin, 1974.

_____. *David Baker Jazz Monograph Series. Charlie Parker: Alto Saxophone.* New York: Shattinger International Music Corp., 1978.

_____. *David Baker Jazz Monograph Series. J. J. Johnson: Trombone.* New York: Shattinger International Music Corp., 1978.

_____. *Ear Training for Jazz Musicians.* 5 volumes. 1. Intervals; 2. Triads/Three Note Sets/Four and Five Note Sets; 3. Seventh Chords/Scales; 4. Major Melodies/Turnarounds/I VI$_7$ Formulae; 5. II V$_7$ Patterns. Lebanon, Indiana: Studio P/R, Inc., 1981.

_____. Giants of Jazz series. See volumes under their individual titles, all of which start with *The Jazz Style of - - -* (fill in name of artist). 6 volumes.

_____. *Improvisational Patterns: The Bebop Era.* 3 volumes. Treble clef and bass clef editions. New York: Charles Colin, 1979.

_____. *Improvisational Patterns: Contemporary Patterns.* Treble clef and bass clef editions. New York: Charles Colin, 1979.

_____. *Improvisational Patterns: Contemporary Patterns.* Treble clef and bass clef editions. New York: Charles Colin, 1979.

_____. *A Jazz Improvisation Method for Stringed Instruments.* 2 volumes. *Volume One: Violin and Viola. Volume Two: Cello and Bass Viol.* Bloomington, Indiana: Frangipani Press, 1976.

_____. *Jazz Pedagogy: A Comprehensive Method of Jazz Education for Teacher and Student.* Bloomington, Indiana: Frangipani Press, 1979.

_____. *The Jazz Style of Clifford Brown: A Musical and Historical Perspective.* Lebanon, Indiana: Studio P/R, Inc., 1982.

_____. *The Jazz Style of Fats Navarro: A Musical and Historical Perspective.* Lebanon, Indiana: Studio P/R, Inc., 1982.

_____. *The Jazz Style of John Coltrane: A Musical and Historical Perspective.* Lebanon, Indiana: Studio P/R, Inc., 1980.

_____. *The Jazz Style of Julian "Cannonball" Adderley: A Musical and Historical Perspective.* Lebanon, Indiana: Studio P/R, Inc., 1980.

_____. *The Jazz Style of Miles Davis: A Musical and Historical Perspective.* Lebanon, Indiana: Studio P/R, Inc., 1980.

_____. *The Jazz Style of Sonny Rollins: A Musical and Historical Perspective.* Lebanon, Indiana: Studio P/R, Inc., 1980.

_____, editor and compiler. *The Monk Montgomery Electric Bass Method* by Monk Montgomery. Edited and compiled by David Baker. Lebanon, Indiana: Studio P/R, Inc.

_____. *A New Approach to Ear Training for the Jazz Musician.* Lebanon, Indiana: Studio P/R, Inc., 1976.

_____. *Techniques of Improvisation. Volume 1: A Method for Developing Improvisational Technique (Based on the Lydian Chromatic Concept by George Russell).* Rev. ed. Bloomington, Indiana: Frangipani Press, 1971.

_____. *Techniques of Improvisation. Volume 2: The II V$_7$ Progression.* Rev. ed. Bloomington, Indiana: Frangipani Press, 1971.

_____. *Techniques of Improvisation. Volume 3: Turnbacks.* Bloomington, Indiana: Frangipani Press, 1971.

_____. *Techniques of Improvisation. Volume 4: Cycles.* Bloomington, Indiana: Frangipani Press, 1971.

Brindle, Reginald Smith. *Serial Composition.* London: Oxford University Press, 1966.

Broudy, Harry S. "A Realistic Philosophy of Music Education." *National Society for the Study of Education Yearbook*, edited by Nelson B. Henry. Chicago: University of Chicago Press, 1958.

Budds, Michael J. *Jazz in the Sixties.* Iowa City, Iowa: University of Iowa Press, 1978.

Burswold, Lee. *Topics in Jazz Piano Improvisation.* Lebanon, Indiana: Studio P/R, Inc., 1980.

Carter, Ron. *Comprehensive Bass Method.*

_____. *Ron Carter's Bass Lines.* Transcribed from volume 6 (*All Bird*) of Jamey Aebersold's series of play-along records (*A New Approach to Jazz Improvisation*).

Chesky, David. *Contemporary Keyboard Exercises.* New York: Charles Colin.

Coker, Jerry. *The Complete Method for Improvisation.* Lebanon, Indiana: Studio P/R, Inc., 1980.

_____. *Improvising Jazz.* Englewood Cliffs, New Jersey: Prentice-Hall, Inc., 1964.

_____. *The Jazz Idiom.* Englewood Cliffs, New Jersey: Prentice-Hall, Inc., 1975.

_____. *Listening to Jazz.* Englewood Cliffs, New Jersey: Prentice-Hall, Inc., 1978.

Coker, Jerry; Casale, Jimmy; Campbell, Gary; and Greene, Jerry. *Patterns for Jazz.* Lebanon, Indiana: Studio P/R, Inc., 1970.

Cooper, Grosvenor W. and Meyer, Leonard B. *The Rhythmic Structure of Music.* Chicago: University of Chicago Press, 1960.

Dallin, Leon. *Techniques of Twentieth Century Composition*. Dubuque, Iowa: Wm. C. Brown Company, 1957.

Dankworth, Avril. *Jazz: An Introduction to Its Musical Basis*. London: Oxford University Press, 1968.

De Johnette, Jack and Perry, Charlie. *The Art of Modern Jazz Drumming*.

De Michael, Don and Dawson, Alan. *A Manual for the Modern Drummer*. Berklee.

Dobbins, Bill. *The Contemporary Jazz Pianist*. 4 volumes. Jamestown, R.I.: GAMT Music Press, 1978.

Garcia, Russell. *The Professional Arranger Composer*. New York: Criterion Music Corp., 1954.

Haerle, Dan. *Jazz Improvisation for Keyboard Players*. 3 volumes. Book One: Basic Concepts. Book Two: Intermediate Concepts. Book Three: Advanced Concepts. Also available with all three volumes in one book. Lebanon, Indiana: Studio P/R, Inc., 1978.

_____. *Jazz/Rock Voicings for the Contemporary Keyboard Player*. Lebanon, Indiana: Studio P/R, Inc., 1974.

_____. *Scales for Jazz Improvisation*. Lebanon, Indiana: Studio P/R, Inc., 1975.

Hindemith, Paul. *A Composer's World*. Garden City, New York: Doubleday & Company/Anchor Books, 1961. Originally published by Harvard University Press, 1952.

Jones, Philly Joe. *Brush Artistry*.

Jost, Ekkehard. *Free Jazz*. Graz: Universal Edition, 1974.

Kennan, Kent. *The Technique of Orchestration*. Englewood Cliffs, New Jersey: Prentice-Hall, Inc., 1952.

Kirk, Willis. *Brush Fire: An Innovative Method for the Development of Brush Technique*. San Francisco: R. and W. Publications, 1981.

Kofsky, Frank. *Black Nationalism and the Revolution in Music*. New York: Pathfinder Press, 1970.

Křenek, Ernst. *Studies in Counterpoint*. New York: Schirmer, 1940.

Laird, Rick. *Improvising Bass Lines*.

Langer, Susanne K. *Feeling and Form*. Scribner's, 1953.

La Porta, John. *Functional Piano for the Improviser*.

_____. *Jazz Ear Training*.

Mason, Thom. *Ear Training for Improvisors*.

Mehegan, John. *Jazz Improvisation*. 4 volumes. *Volume 1: Tonal and Rhythmic Principles. Volume 2: Jazz Rhythm and the Improvised Line. Volume 3: Swing and Early Progressive Piano Styles. Volume 4: Contemporary Piano Styles*. New York: Watson-Guptill Publications.

Miller, Harold. *Bebop Bass*.

Nelson, Oliver. *Patterns for Saxophone*. Hollywood: Nolsen Music, 1966. Currently published under the title *Patterns for Jazz*.

Pepper, Stephen C. *Aesthetic Quality*. Scribner's, 1938.

_____. *The Basis of Criticism in the Arts*. Harvard University Press, 1949.

Pratt, Carroll C. *The Meaning of Music*. McGraw-Hill, 1931.

Reid, Rufus. *The Evolving Bassist*. Teaneck, New Jersey: Myriad Limited, 1974.

_____. *Evolving Upward*. Teaneck, New Jersey: Myriad Limited, 1977.

_____. *Rufus Reid Bass Lines*. Exactly as recorded. Transcribed from Volumes 1 & 3 of Jamey Aebersold's play-along series. Transcribed by David Leonhardt and Ken Slone. Edited by Jamey Aebersold. New Albany, Indiana: Jamey Aebersold, 1980.

Ricker, Ramon. *Pentatonic Scales for Jazz Improvisations*. Lebanon, Indiana: Studio P/R, Inc., 1975.

_____. *The Ramon Ricker Improvisation Series*. Series volumes listed as follows: volume 1: *The Beginning Improviser*; volume 2: *The Developing Improviser*; volume 3: *All Blues*; volume 4: *II-V-I Progressions*; volume 5: *Jerome Kern's Great Jazz Songs*. Lebanon, Indiana: Studio P/R, Inc.

Russell, George. *The Lydian Chromatic Concept of Tonal Organization for Improvisation*. New York: Concept Publishing Co., 1959.

Schaeffer, Don and Colin, Charles. *Encyclopedia of Scales*. New York: New Sounds in Modern Music, 1964.

Slonimsky, Nicholas. *A Thesaurus of Scales*.

Stein, Leon. *Structure and Style*. Summy-Birchard, 1962.

Toch, Ernest. *Shaping Forces in Music*. Criterion, 1948.

# BIOGRAPHICAL NOTES

**DAVID NATHANIEL BAKER**—author, composer, arranger, instrumentalist, and teacher—is a gifted and versatile musician equally at home in all worlds of music.

Born December 21, 1931 in Indianapolis, Indiana, Baker first established his musical reputation as a brilliant jazz trombonist. He worked with the big bands of Stan Kenton, Maynard Ferguson, Buddy Johnson, Lionel Hampton, and Quincy Jones and with combos led by Wes Montgomery, Harold Land, Charles Tyler, and most notably, George Russell. Currently, Baker performs on cello.

Baker holds the B.M.E. and M.M.E. degrees from Indiana University. He studied trombone with Thomas Beversdorf, William Adam, J. J. Johnson, Bob Brookmeyer, and others; cello with Leopold Teraspulsky, Jules Eskin, Norma Woodbury, Helga Winold, Janos Starker, and others; and theory and composition with George Russell, William Russo, John Lewis, Gunther Schuller, Bernard Heiden, and others.

Baker received a *down beat* Hall of Fame Scholarship Award in 1959 and won *down beat's* New Star Award: Trombone in the 1962 International Jazz Critics Poll. In 1981 he was the recipient of the National Association of Jazz Educators Hall of Fame Award.

In the non-jazz realm Baker has been a member of the Indiana University Philharmonic and Opera orchestras and the Wind and Brass Ensemble; the Butler University Orchestra, Band, and Brass Ensemble; and the Indianapolis Civic Orchestra. He has made solo appearances with and has had his compositions performed by the New York Philharmonic, among many orchestras. Artists who have performed Baker's compositions include Josef Gingold, Janos Starker, Ruggerio Ricci, James Pellerite, Gary Karr, Bertram Turetzky, and Harvey Phillips.

David Baker is currently Professor of Music at the Indiana University School of Music and is Chairman of the Jazz Department, supervising one of the most important jazz studies programs in the U.S. He also travels extensively in his various roles as clinician, lecturer, performer, and conductor.